ENDANGERED WILDLIFE

Anita Ganeri

Silver Dolphin

Silver Dolphin Books
An imprint of Printers Row Publishing Group
A division of Readerlink Distribution Services, LLC
10350 Barnes Canyon Road, Suite 100, San Diego, CA 92121
www.silverdolphinbooks.com

Printers Row Publishing Group is a division of Readerlink Distribution Services, LLC.
Silver Dolphin Books is a registered trademark of Readerlink Distribution Services, LLC.

All notations of errors or omissions should be addressed to Silver Dolphin Books, Editorial Department,
at the above address. All other correspondence (author inquiries, permissions) concerning the content of
this book should be addressed to:
Hodder & Stoughton Limited
Carmelite House
50 Victoria Embankment
London EC4Y 0DZ

ISBN: 978-1-64517-535-3
Manufactured, printed, and assembled in Dongguan City, Guang Dong Province, China.
First printing, December 2020. SWT/12/20
24 23 22 21 20 1 2 3 4 5

The material in this book has previously been published in the following titles:
Endangered Wildlife: Rescuing Amphibians   *Endangered Wildlife: Rescuing Mammals*
Endangered Wildlife: Rescuing Birds   *Endangered Wildlife: Rescuing Ocean Life*
Endangered Wildlife: Rescuing Insects and Invertebrates *Endangered Wildlife: Rescuing Reptiles*

Picture credits:
Every effort has been made to contact copyright holders for the images in this book.
If you are a copyright holder of any uncredited image herein, please contact Hodder & Stoughton at the address above.

Alamy: AvalonPhotoshot 33b,50,157; Bill Bachman 139; Steve Bentley 135t; Blickwinkel 37tcr, 46, 108; Joe Blossom 37tl, 40; David Boag 168;
Geraldine Buckley 107t; Mark Conlin 121tcr, 137t; Jean-Paul Ferrero/Auscape Int. 37br, 49b; GM Photos 8b, 68b,149cr,167b; anthony grote
121cl,128–9; Fred Grover Jr back cover c,4; Hemis 93cr, 96, 97b; Juston Hofman 93bl, 103t; Imagebroker 15t; Images & Stories 135c; John
Insull 153; Mauritius Images GmbH 9tcl; 14; Minden Pictures 8r, 93 bcl, 93bcr, 100–101, 112;Carl Monopol 59; Nature and Science 93tl, 116;
Doug Peebles Photography 161; Moreley Read 61; Rweisswald 149tc, 155t; Cheryl Schneider 35,57t; Nick Upton 36b; volkerpreusser 15b; Song
Wen/Xinhua 39. **Bridgeman Images:** Royal Albert Memorial Museum, Exeter 97t. **FLPA Images:** Stephen Belcher 71; Michael & Patricia Fogden
149bcr,156;Gregory Guida/Biosphotos 149tcl, 152; Michel Gunther/Biosphoto 149tcr,171t; Martin Hale 66cr, 66b, 67; Christian Hatter/Imagebroker
170–1; Richard Herrmann 123; David Hosking 86b; Sebastian Kennerknecht 141b; Albert Lieal/Minden Pictures 47; Flip Micklin 122b; Pete
Oxford/Minden back cover b,145; Norbert Wu 133. **Nature PL:** Oriol Alama ny 45t; Karl Amman 10b; Ingo Arndt 63, 66bc, 80, 81t, 81b,167t;
Eric Baccega 66 bcl, 82; Miles Barton 164b; Nigel Bean 8l; Emanuelle Biggi 7, 9bc, 16t; Clay Bolt 105; Mattias Breiter141t; Barrie Britton 166;
John Cancalosi 43b, 68t; Mark Cardavine 16b, 20b, 121tl, 126b; Bernard Castelein 154–155; Claudio Contreras back cover t,66cl,69,149tl, 150c ;
Christophe Courteau 149bcl, 164–5; Stephen Dalton 37cl, 42, 93tcl, 98, 99t, 99b; Adrian Davies 148t; Suzi Eszterhas front cover tr, 23, 121cr.,140;
Chris & Monique Fallows 120b; David Fleetham 121 bcl, 124; Jurgen Freuend 125b, 129, 150bt, 151b;Nick Garbutt 9bcr, 20t, 21, 66bl, 72, 73;
Laurent Geslin 26b; Patricio Robes Gil 75; Chris Gomershall/2020Vision 92; Daniel Heuclin 37tr, 38, 85; Michael Hutchinson 64t; Alex Hyde 37tcl,
52, 53; Steven Kazlowski 25b;Tim Lamman 147,149br, 160; Mark MacEwen 17, 149tr, 162; Remi Masson 121br; Vladimir Medvedev 9tcr; 28;
Remi Masson 142; Steven David Miller 49t; Mark Moffet 117; Alex Mustard 120, 121tr, 126–7,132; Nature Production 66tc,86–87c; Pete Oxford
43t, 79t; Doug Perrine 121cl, 128b, 134; Tony Phelps 169t; Michael Pitts 162b; Todd Pusser 119, 121 bcr,144; Moreley Read 37bl, 60; Andy
Rouse 11,13t, 25t; Tui de Roy front cover tl, 66tl, 66bcr, 70, 78–9, 78b, 149cl,149bl, 172, 173t; Cyril Ruoso 9t,12 31,66tcl,83,88, 163; Andy
Sands 149bc, 158, 159t, 159c, 169b; Francois Savigny 165b; Roland Seitre 9clb,9bl, 26t, 27, 32, 33c,41,66br, 84c, 84b, 121bl, 130, 131; Anup
Shah 9crb; 9bcl, 22t, 22b,30t, 30b, 154t ; Yuri Sheibnev 29; Igor Shpilenok 77; Paul D Stewart 64b; David Tipling 92b; Nick Upton 143t,143b;
Dave Watts 9br, 18, 19t; Theo Webb front cover bl,9tr,10; Wild Wonders of Europe 9tl,24; Rod Williams 37cr, 56; Tony Wu 127b; Solvin Zanki
37tc, 44,45c; Jean Pierre Zwaenepoel 76b. **Shutterstock:** Auscape/UIG 121tc, 138l; barmalini 125t; Nic Bothma/EPA 37bcr, 51b, 136; feather
collector 66tr,74; FotoMonkey 173c; Anton Gvozdikov 160b; Industry & Travel 102–103; David W. Leindecker 37bc, 58; Shane Meyers Photography
front cover br; Vincent Mounier 51t; James D Morgan 95t; Tracey Nearmy/EPA 91, 93br, 94, 95b; Dan Olsen 93tr, 109; Jay Pierstorff 148b;Arda
Savascioguillari 111; Damian Ryszawy 113; Wang Li Quang 66tcr, 76c. **Other contributers:** Michèle Lemonnier-Darcemont: 93tc,110.Dr John
Measey: 37bcl, 55. Dr Warren Tarboton: 93bc,106; Katy Thompson: 93tcr, 114, 115.USFWS/Peter Pearsall PD: 93cl, 104. VIVA Vaquita T.A.
Jefferson 121cr, 122.Wikimedia Commons/Dr Raju Kasambe CCASA 3: 89. Wildlife Conservation Society/Lukje Groskin: 66t.

Poster image: Theo Webb (Nature Picture Library)

CONTENTS

BIRDS

INSECTS AND INVERTEBRATES

OCEAN LIFE

REPTILES

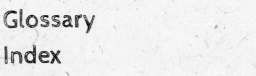

WILDLIFE IN DANGER

Extinction is when a plant or animal dies out. Scientists think that more than 99 percent of all the **species** that have ever lived on Earth are extinct. In the past this was due to massive natural events, such as asteroid strikes. Today, it's largely due to human behavior that many creatures' futures are so uncertain.

Danger Rating

The wildlife in this book have been given a status rating, set by the IUCN (International Union for the Conservation of Nature). This rating is based on how close to extinction an animal is thought to be. Most of the wildlife in this book are critically **endangered**, endangered, or **vulnerable**. Critically endangered means that they face an extremely high risk of becoming extinct in the wild. Endangered means that they are very likely to become extinct. Vulnerable means that they will probably become endangered unless the threats facing them can be reduced.

Upsetting the Balance

Planet Earth is home to an amazing variety of animals and plants. This variety is known as **biodiversity**, and it is the result of millions of years of **evolution**. If animals or plants become extinct, there is a loss of biodiversity. In the natural world, the species in a **habitat** rely on each other for their survival. The loss of even one species in a food chain can have a disastrous domino effect.

Make a Difference

You can get involved to help the animals you'll see in this book! Visit these websites to learn more about how to get involved in their work to save endangered wildlife:

www.iucnredlist.org
The IUCN (International Union for Conservation of Nature) Red List of endangered animals and plants is a great place to start.

www.worldwildlife.org/species
The WWF (World Wildlife Fund) has information about endangered animals and conservation projects.

ENDANGERED
MAMMALS

MAMMALS IN DANGER

Today, around a quarter of the world's mammals face extinction.

This chapter looks at some of the most endangered mammals. They have been chosen to show the different threats they face—from habitat loss or illegal poaching to hunting for their meat or body parts. The good news is that many governments and conservationists are working hard to save these mammals—and their homes—before it is too late.

Przewalski's horse came close to extinction, but some were bred in captivity and reintroduced to the wild.

A polar bear catches a seal to eat as part of an Arctic food chain.

WHAT ARE MAMMALS?

- **Vertebrates**
- **Warm-blooded**
- Give birth to live young
- Young feeds on milk provided by its mother
- Often covered in hair

LOCATOR MAP: MAMMALS

Giant panda

Polar bear

Wild Bactrian camel

Amur leopard

Tiger

Iberian lynx

Baird's tapir

Western lowland gorilla

Orangutan

Aye-aye

Northern hairy-nosed wombat

Black rhinoceros

TIGER

Famous for its stripes, the tiger is one of the largest of the big cats. It lives in forests and mangrove swamps, where its stripes provide camouflage as it stalks its food. A fierce hunter, the tiger has powerful jaws and sharp teeth for killing its prey.

Tigers in Trouble

Tigers once roamed large parts of Asia, but in the last one hundred years they have lost around 95 percent of their habitat. The Bali, Javan, and Caspian tigers are already extinct. The rest—the Siberian, South China, Sumatran, Indochinese, Malayan, and Bengal tigers—are in danger of dying out.

A Bengal tiger will live for eight to ten years in the wild.

Tiger skins, and other animal parts, on sale in Myanmar.

Habitat Loss

Habitat loss remains a major threat, as forests are cleared for farmland and homes, while mangrove swamps are being destroyed by flooding and erosion. As their habitat shrinks and prey becomes harder to find, tigers turn to livestock for food. This puts the tigers in conflict with local farmers. Tigers are also hunted for their skin and bones, which are used in traditional medicine, despite laws banning this trade.

Save the Tiger

At the beginning of the twentieth century, there were around 100,000 tigers. A century later, numbers had dropped as low as 3,200. Since then, numbers have risen to around 3,890, thanks to work by conservation groups and governments. In India, for example, Project Tiger works with local people to reduce tiger attacks and has a Tiger Protection Force to catch poachers. In 2010, Project Tx2 was launched by the WWF in the thirteen countries in which tigers are still found. Its aim is to double the number of wild tigers by 2022.

A female Bengal tiger with her cub.

VITAL STATS

Scientific name: *Panthera tigris*

Body length: 7–10 ft.

Weight: 220–660 lbs.

Diet: Deer, wild pigs

Numbers in the wild: Around 3,890

Status: Endangered

Location: Asia
(*range* marked in red below)

Wild Fact Tigers are famous for their stripes, but no two tigers have the same stripe pattern. Like human fingerprints, the patterns are all different.

GIANT PANDA

Giant pandas belong to the bear family. They have large, stocky bodies, with striking black-and-white coats. Once widespread across eastern and southern China, giant pandas now live in a few patches of bamboo forest on remote mountains.

Fussy Eater

About 99 percent of a giant panda's diet is made up of bamboo. The rest is made up of other plants and even birds and rodents. Bamboo is tough to digest. To get enough nourishment, an adult panda must spend most of its time eating—up to 40 lbs. of food a day. Pandas use specially adapted wrist bones as thumbs for gripping the bamboo stalks as they eat.

Habitat Destruction

Because pandas rely so much on bamboo, they are very sensitive to changes in their habitat. Bamboo naturally dies back every twenty years or so. In the past, the pandas simply found another patch, but this is no longer possible because of habitat loss. Large areas of forest have been cleared for timber and farming, leaving only small, scattered areas for the pandas.

A panda feeding on its favorite meal of bamboo.

Some pandas are now bred and studied in captivity.

VITAL STATS

Scientific name:
Ailuropoda melanoleuca
Body length: More than 4 ft.
Weight: 220–330 lbs.
Diet: Mostly bamboo
Numbers in the wild: Around 1,870
Status: Vulnerable
Location: China

Panda Protection

Since the 1960s, the giant panda has been the symbol of the WWF. The WWF has been working with the Chinese government and conservation groups to help protect the panda. A **captive-breeding program**, together with the setting up of special forest reserves, have helped increase the number of pandas in the wild from around 1,000 in the 1970s to around 1,870 today.

Wild Fact A giant panda's gut is lined with an extra-thick layer of slimy mucus. This protects the gut from damage that could be caused by sharp splinters of bamboo.

WILD BACTRIAN CAMEL

Superbly adapted to life in the harsh Gobi Desert, wild Bactrian camels can survive for days without drinking, and store fat in their humps for when food is scarce. Their thick fur keeps them warm in the freezing winter, but is shed during the summer heat.

Camel Survivors

There may only be around 1,000 wild Bactrian camels left. They are found in four remote locations in northwest China and southwest Mongolia. The largest group lives in part of the Gobi Desert in China.

VITAL STATS

Scientific name: *Camelus ferus*

Height at shoulder: 6–8 ft.

Weight: 1,320–2,210 lbs.

Diet: Thorny plants and shrubs

Numbers in the wild: Fewer than 1,000

Status: Critically endangered

Location: China, Mongolia

Camels at Risk

For centuries, wild Bactrian camels have been hunted for their meat and skins. In addition, they are losing their remaining habitat as it is taken over for mining and livestock. Experts estimate a massive 80 percent drop in their numbers over the next fifty years.

Together with the Wild Camel Protection Foundation, the Chinese and Mongolian governments are working to protect the remaining camels, and two special reserves have been established. A captive-breeding program has also been set up in Mongolia—the only one of its kind in the world.

A herd of wild Bactrian camels in Mongolia.

Wild Fact

During a sandstorm, a wild Bactrian camel's double row of extra-long eyelashes and long, slit-like nostrils help to keep the sand out of its nose and eyes.

Camels have adapted to survive the arid conditions of the Gobi Desert.

BLACK RHINOCEROS

With its huge armor-plated body and pointed horns, the black rhino looks like a creature straight out of prehistory. This magnificent animal lives in grasslands, deserts, and forests in Africa, where it browses on leaves and woody plants.

Rare Rhinos

Once found across large parts of sub-Saharan Africa, black rhinos are now extremely rare. They are mostly found in South Africa, Namibia, Zimbabwe, and Kenya. By 1993, black rhino numbers had decreased from around 65,000 to an all-time low of around 2,300 animals. Thanks to conservation efforts and greater protection, the population has gradually increased to around 5,000.

A black rhino grazing in the Maasai Mara National Park in Kenya.

Guards patrol the parks to protect the rhinos from poachers.

Hunted Down

In the past, black rhinos were hunted for their meat and hide. Their habitat was also cleared to make space for farmland and settlements. The main threat that they still face is poaching for their valuable horn. Rhino horn is used in traditional medicine and for making elaborate handles for ceremonial daggers.

Precious Horns

Despite being illegal, the trade in rhino horn continues to grow. Many wild rhinos now live in heavily protected reserves. Some rhinos have their horns deliberately, and painlessly, removed by veterinarians to make the animals worthless to poachers.

VITAL STATS

Scientific name: *Diceros bicornis*

Body length: 10–12 ft.

Weight: 1,760–3,090 lbs.

Diet: Leaves, twigs

Numbers in the wild: Around 4,880

Status: Critically endangered

Location: Eastern and southern Africa

A black rhino that has had its horn removed by vets.

Wild Fact Both black and white rhinos are really gray, but you can tell them apart by their lips. Black rhinos have hooklike upper lips that they use for gripping food. White rhinos have square lips.

NORTHERN HAIRY-NOSED WOMBAT

One of the world's rarest mammals, the northern hairy-nosed wombat has a stocky body with silver-gray fur, short, strong legs, and a short tail. It uses the strong claws on its front legs like spades for digging burrows, where it rests and breeds.

Wild Wombats

Today, there are fewer than 200 northern hairy-nosed wombats left in the wild. Their natural habitat is dry grassland and eucalyptus woodland, much of which has been lost to farmland or destroyed by wildfires, floods, and droughts. The wombats are also hunted by dingoes and have found themselves in competition for food with farmers' livestock.

A northern hairy-nosed wombat in Epping Forest National Park, Australia.

A wombat being released from a trap, after scientists have checked it.

VITAL STATS

Scientific name: *Lasiorhinus krefftii*

Body length: More than 3 ft.

Weight: Around 71 lbs.

Diet: Grasses

Numbers in the wild: Fewer than 200

Status: Critically endangered

Location: Northeast Australia

Wombat Watch

Most of the surviving wombats live in Epping Forest National Park in Queensland, Australia. To protect them, the park is not open to the public and the wombats are surrounded by a 7-ft.-high fence to keep **predators** out. The wombats are closely monitored by rangers and scientists, who use remote cameras to photograph them.

Because there are so few wombats, there is a real danger that a single fire or flood could wipe the whole group and species out. In 2009, several wombats were flown from Epping Forest to the Richard Underwood Nature Refuge to establish another **colony** and reduce the risk. The new colony is doing well, with the first baby born in 2017.

Wild Fact Like kangaroos, wombats are **marsupials**, with pouches where their babies grow. But the wombat's pouch opens backward so that it does not fill with earth as it digs its burrow.

AYE-AYE

Found in the forests of Madagascar, the aye-aye is a small mammal with extraordinary looks. It has a thick, gray-brown coat flecked with white and a long, bushy tail. Its ears are large and bat-like. It feeds on fruit and insect **larvae**.

Unlucky Lemur

The aye-aye is a type of lemur—Madagascar's best-known animals. Along with 80 percent of the island's wildlife, the aye-aye is found nowhere else on Earth. Today, it is at serious risk of becoming extinct, as its home is destroyed for timber and to make space for farming and settlement. Aye-ayes are also killed by local people who believe that the animals bring bad luck.

The aye-aye's large eyes help it to see in the dark.

Wild Fact Aye-ayes have very long, twiglike middle fingers for tapping on tree bark to locate insect larvae. They then tear the bark open with their teeth and scoop the larvae out.

A captive aye-aye with its keeper.

VITAL STATS

Scientific name: *Daubentonia madagascariensis*

Length: (body) 1 ft.
(tail) 1–2 ft.

Weight: 4–7 lbs.

Diet: Fruit, insect larvae

Numbers in the wild: Unknown

Status: Endangered

Location: Madagascar

Living Alone

The aye-aye is **nocturnal** and spends the day sleeping in a twig nest high up in the trees. It is also quite solitary and usually lives on its own. This makes it difficult to monitor, and scientists do not know how many aye-ayes are left in the wild but believe that their numbers are falling fast. Unless their habitat is saved, numbers may drop by half in the next ten to twenty years.

Saving the Aye-aye

On Madagascar, aye-ayes are protected in several national parks. There are also aye-ayes in zoos around the world, where they form part of captive-breeding programs. Since the 1990s, Jersey Zoo has been working with the government of Madagascar to protect the aye-aye. So far, eight babies have been born at the zoo.

ORANGUTAN

Orangutans are large apes with shaggy, brownish-red fur. Ideally suited for their life in the rain forest, orangutans have very long arms for swinging through the trees and hook-shaped hands and feet for gripping branches.

A young male orangutan uses his long arms to swing through the trees.

On the Brink

Once found across Southeast Asia, today orangutans only live on the islands of Borneo and Sumatra, and are close to becoming extinct. There may be as few as 7,500 orangutans left on Sumatra.

Some orangutans are killed for meat by hunters or if they wander into villages. Others, especially young animals, may be captured for the illegal pet trade. But the greatest threat is the loss of the orangutan's rain forest habitat, which is being cleared for logging, gold mining, and palm oil **plantations**.

Wild Fact At night, orangutans sleep in nests in the trees. They build the nests from branches and twigs. If it is raining, they add a cover of leaves and also use leaves as pillows.

Nursery Care

Orangutans breed very slowly—females only have one baby about every eight years. This means that even a small fall in numbers could put them at serious risk. The apes are protected by law, and urgent efforts are being made to save their rain forest habitat. Special "nurseries" have also been set up for orphan orangutans. Here, they learn skills, such as climbing, that they need in order to return to the forest.

VITAL STATS

Scientific name: *Pongo pygmaeus* (Bornean); *Pongo abelii* (Sumatran)

Body length: 4–6 ft.

Weight: 77–180 lbs.

Diet: Fruit, leaves, shoots

Numbers in the wild: Around 100,000 (Bornean); around 7,500 (Sumatran)

Status: Critically endangered

Location: Sumatra, Borneo

A young orangutan with a conservation worker at an orangutan care center in Borneo.

POLAR BEAR

The largest living land carnivore, a male polar bear can grow up to 9 ft. long and weigh up to 1,320 lbs. It is brilliantly adapted to its freezing Arctic home, with a thick, white fur coat for warmth, strong limbs, and large front paws for swimming.

A polar bear hunting on the sea ice in northern Norway.

Seal Hunters

A polar bear's favorite prey is ringed seals. It waits by a seal's breathing hole, then pounces when the seal surfaces for air, or hunts them in their icy dens. Using its superb sense of smell, a bear can detect prey nearly a mile away and more than 3 ft. under the ice.

Wild Fact To stop them from slipping on the ice, polar bears have sharp claws like ice picks and small bumps on the soles of their feet that work like suction cups.

Shrinking Ice

Polar bears are found across the Arctic. They live on the ice near the coast, where there are plenty of seals to eat. Today, their habitat is under threat from **climate change**. As Earth warms and the sea ice shrinks, the bears are in danger of losing their hunting grounds. This is particularly devastating for pregnant females, who need to build up stores of fat to live off when they are nursing their cubs.

A female polar bear with her cub.

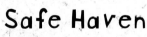

Polar bears are superb swimmers.

VITAL STATS

Scientific name: *Ursus maritimus*
Body length: 6–9 ft.
Weight: 440–1,320 lbs.
Diet: Mostly seals
Numbers in the wild: 20–25,000
Status: Vulnerable
Location: Arctic

Safe Haven

If **global warming** continues at the present rate, it is predicted that the summer sea ice will have disappeared from most of the Arctic by 2040. Only one place may still have ice: the so-called Last Ice Area in Greenland and Canada. Conservationists are planning to protect this region as a rare safe haven for polar bears and other animals.

IBERIAN LYNX

The Iberian lynx is a medium-size wild cat with a spotted coat, long legs, short tail, and small head with long whiskers and tufted ears. It is mainly nocturnal, coming out at dusk to hunt for rabbits to eat.

A female lynx with her cub, which was born in captivity.

Lynx Recovery

At the beginning of the twenty-first century, the Iberian lynx was on the verge of extinction, with as few as ninety animals left in the wild. Today, thanks to the hard work of conservationists, their numbers have risen to around 400.

Rabbit Hunters

A skillful hunter, the lynx specializes in catching rabbits, which make up 90 percent of its diet. Recently, disease wiped out large numbers of rabbits, meaning that the lynx has had to compete fiercely with other animals for prey. Many lynx are also killed on the roads or caught in illegal traps set by poachers, who hunt them for their fur and meat.

A wild Iberian lynx carrying its rabbit prey.

Lynx Management

Protected reserves have been set up where conservationists use cameras and radio collars to monitor the lynx. In some places, underground tunnels have been built so that lynx can cross busy roads. Rabbit numbers are carefully managed to make sure that the lynx have enough food. Lynx are also being bred in captivity for reintroduction into the wild.

VITAL STATS

Scientific name: *Lynx pardinus*

Body length: 2–3 ft.

Weight: 11–33 lbs.

Diet: Mostly rabbits

Numbers in the wild: Around 400

Status: Endangered

Location: Portugal, Spain

A conservationist examines an Iberian lynx at the Doñana Breeding Station in Andalusia, Spain.

Wild Fact No one is sure why a lynx has hairy ear tufts. The hairs may help to direct sounds into its ears, making it easier for the lynx to locate prey.

AMUR LEOPARD

Found only in two remote forest regions of eastern Russia and northeastern China, the Amur leopard is one of the rarest big cats. By 2007, numbers had dropped to around thirty-five leopards. Today, that number has slowly grown to around seventy.

Leopard Life and Death

Amur leopards are nocturnal. During the day, they rest in caves or among thick vegetation, coming out at dawn and dusk to hunt for deer and wild boar. They are well suited to the harsh climate they live in. Their fur coats grow longer and thicker in winter for warmth.

A very rare sighting of a wild Amur leopard in the far east of Russia.

Beautiful Fur

Amur leopards were once much more widespread, but were hunted almost to extinction for their beautiful coats and for their bones, which are used in traditional medicine. Their habitat has also been destroyed by logging, forest fires, and clearance for roads, factories, and farms. Today, there are so few left that a large fire could wipe them out.

Scientists fit a radio collar to a leopard to track it.

Leopard Rescue

As the leopards' habitat vanishes, so do the animals it preys on, such as deer and wild boar. Conservationists are working to set up protected areas, where the numbers of prey animals can be carefully controlled. They also carry out anti-poaching controls and are helping to train local firefighters to put out deadly forest fires. Many fires are started by local farmers to clear their fields, with devastating results for the leopards.

VITAL STATS

Scientific name:
Panthera pardus orientalis
Length: (body) 4–5 ft.
(tail) 3 ft.
Weight: 55–110 lbs.
Diet: Deer, wild boar
Numbers in the wild: Around 70
Status: Critically endangered
Location: Russia, China

Wild Fact Amur leopards have huge, furry tails that they can wrap around themselves like scarves to keep warm.

WESTERN LOWLAND GORILLA

Living in rain forests across western Africa, the western lowland gorilla forms small family groups, made up of an older male, several females, and their young. It mostly lives on the ground, but will climb trees to reach fruit and to build a nest to sleep in.

Gorilla Danger

Over the last twenty-five years, the number of western lowland gorillas left in the wild has fallen by more than 60 percent. The main threats facing these apes are habitat loss, poaching, and disease. Their forest home is being cleared at an alarming rate to make space for farmland, and this makes it easier for poachers to find and kill the gorillas. Young gorillas are also taken for the illegal pet trade.

A group of western lowland gorillas feeding on rotten wood.

A magnificent male gorilla in Dzanga-Sangha Protected Area in the Central African Republic.

Bushmeat

"Bushmeat" from gorillas is eaten by local people and is highly prized as food and as a source of income. Part of the conservation effort to save the gorillas is to try to find alternatives to bushmeat, such as growing more crops or raising more fish and livestock.

A vet examines a five-year-old gorilla at a reintroduction project in Batéké **Plateau** National Park in Gabon.

VITAL STATS

Scientific name:
Gorilla gorilla gorilla

Body length: 5–6 ft.

Weight: 150–400 lbs.

Diet: Mostly fruit

Numbers in the wild: 100–250,000

Status: Critically endangered

Location: Western Africa

Deadly Disease

Disease is another serious danger to these gorillas. It is estimated that between 1992 and 2007, around a third of western lowland gorillas were killed by the highly **infectious** Ebola virus. Scientists are now working on a **vaccine** that could protect gorillas and chimps from this deadly disease.

Wild Fact Adult male western lowland gorillas are called silverbacks for the streak of silvery-white hair on their back.

31

BAIRD'S TAPIR

Baird's tapirs were once found across Central America. Today, so much of their rain forest habitat has been destroyed that they only survive in a few pockets of forest and are already extinct across much of their former home.

A Baird's tapir in Belize.

Tapir Tracks

Tapirs have barrel-shaped bodies and short legs. Their long, flexible upper lips look like a short version of an elephant's trunk. Tapirs **forage** for food at night, following well-trodden paths through the undergrowth.

VITAL STATS

Scientific name: *Tapirus bairdii*

Body length: 6–8 ft.

Weight: 330–660 lbs.

Diet: Leaves, seeds, fruit

Numbers in the wild: Unknown

Status: Endangered

Location: Central America

Skillful Swimmers

Good swimmers, tapirs stay close to rivers and streams. They use the water for cooling down on hot days and for hiding from danger.

Tapir Threats

The main threat facing Baird's tapirs is loss of habitat. Huge areas of Central American rain forest have been cleared for cattle ranches, roads, and homes. Some tapirs are hunted, while others die from diseases caught from **domestic** animals brought into the cleared forest.

In most of Central America, tapirs are protected by law, but these laws are often broken. Unless their habitat can be saved, they are at serious risk of dying out. Conservationists are now focusing on managing how logging is carried out. If it is done carefully—and sustainably—leaving patches of habitat behind, there may still be hope for the tapirs.

Wild Fact Newborn tapirs have reddish-brown coats with white stripes and spots. These markings help to camouflage them among the dappled light of the forest.

ENDANGERED
AMPHIBIANS

AMPHIBIANS IN DANGER

Today, around a third of the world's **amphibians** are facing extinction.

This chapter looks at some of the most endangered amphibians, showing the different threats they face, including widespread disease and illegal hunting. Thankfully, many people are working hard to increase amphibian populations before it's too late.

The golden toad from Costa Rica is now extinct around the world.

This palmate newt was found in a bottle trap placed in a pond as part of a conservation project to protect its habitat.

WHAT ARE AMPHIBIANS?

- Vertebrates
- Live on land or in water
- Born with **gills** to breathe underwater, but develop lungs as adults
- Most hatch from eggs
- **Cold-blooded**

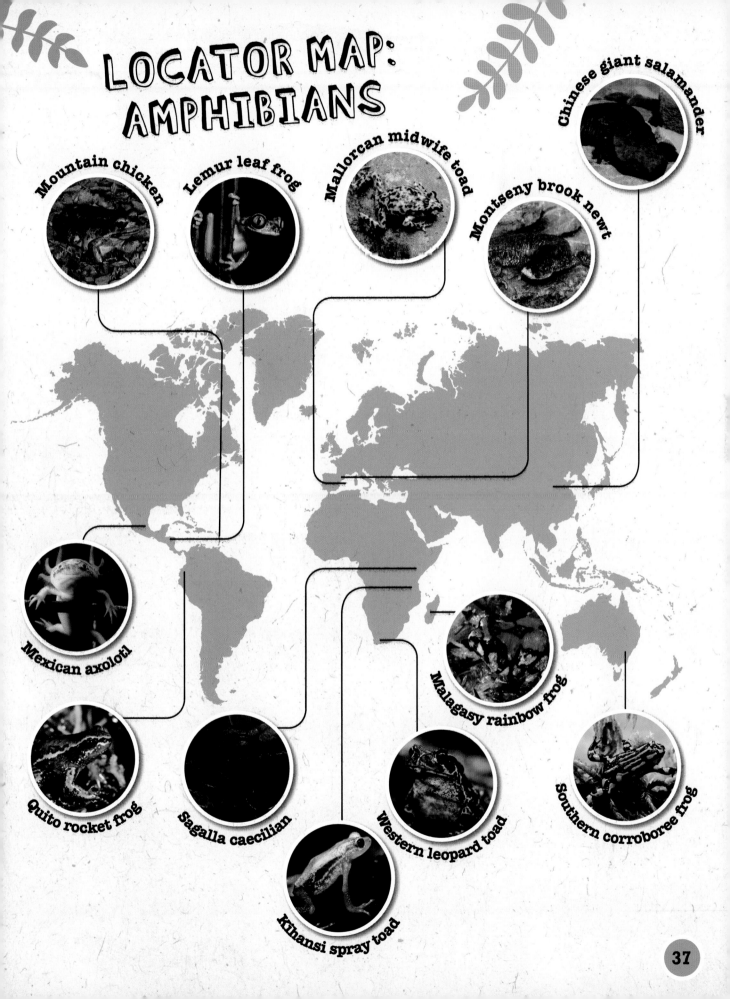

LOCATOR MAP: AMPHIBIANS

Chinese giant salamander

Mountain chicken

Lemur leaf frog

Mallorcan midwife toad

Montseny brook newt

Mexican axolotl

Quito rocket frog

Sagalla caecilian

Kihansi spray toad

Western leopard toad

Malagasy rainbow frog

Southern corroboree frog

CHINESE GIANT SALAMANDER

A salamander is a lizard-like amphibian. The Chinese giant salamander is the largest salamander in the world, growing up to 6 ft. long. It was once widespread in cold, fast-flowing mountain streams, but it is now endangered.

The Chinese giant salamander is also known as the baby fish because it makes noises like a baby crying.

Sensitive Salamander

The Chinese giant salamander usually hunts at night, finding its prey by touch and smell. It feeds on insects, **reptiles**, **mollusks**, crayfish, worms, and even smaller salamanders. From late August to September, large groups of salamanders gather at nesting sites along riverbanks. The female lays up to 500 eggs in a rocky crevice, then the male guards them for about three months until they hatch.

Giant Threats

The giant salamander is now very rare. Its habitat is being rapidly destroyed by soil erosion from **deforestation**, dam building, which alters the flow of streams and rivers, and chemicals used in farming. But the greatest threat comes from humans who consider the salamander's flesh to be a delicacy and use its body parts in traditional medicine.

Wild Fact The Chinese giant salamander is well adapted to its aquatic lifestyle. Unlike fish, it does not have gills for breathing, but takes in oxygen through its moist, wrinkled skin.

Feeding giant salamanders at a captive-breeding facility in China.

Saving the Salamander

Hunting giant salamanders is now illegal, and China has nature reserves where salamanders and their habitat are protected. A successful captive-breeding program has been started, with the aim of releasing adults back into the wild. There are also farms across China where large numbers of salamanders are raised, legally, for their meat. A growing problem, however, is the number of farmed salamanders escaping into the wild, where they spread diseases that the remaining wild salamanders are not **immune** to.

MOUNTAIN CHICKEN

The mountain chicken is a large frog, found on only two Caribbean islands. Hunted for its meat, its fleshy legs are said to taste like chicken, which is how it got its unusual name.

This mountain chicken was bred in captivity, but has been released into the wild in the Caribbean.

Cunning Colors

One of the world's largest species of frog, the mountain chicken can measure up to 8.5 in. long. It lives mainly near forest springs and streams, where its mottled brown coloring provides the perfect camouflage for hunting. The frog sits still, waiting for prey, such as crickets and millipedes, which it swallows whole.

Deadly Disease

Over the last twenty years, the number of mountain chickens has plummeted. They have lost large areas of habitat to farming, tourism, and construction. Since 1995, an active volcano on the island of Montserrat has wiped out whole groups of frogs. Tens of thousands have also been killed for their meat, though hunting them is now banned. A worse threat now faces the frogs. In 2009, a deadly **fungal** disease called **chytridiomycosis**, or chytrid for short, broke out on the islands. It attacked the frogs' skin, which they breathe through. A staggering 99 percent of mountain chickens were wiped out.

A scientist monitoring a mountain chicken at a wildlife park.

VITAL STATS

Scientific name:
Leptodactylus fallax

Body length: Up to 8.5 in.
(larger female)

Weight: Around 2 lbs.

Diet: Insects, spiders, worms, snails, centipedes, small frogs, snakes

Numbers in the wild: Approx. 100

Status: Critically endangered

Location: Dominica, Montserrat

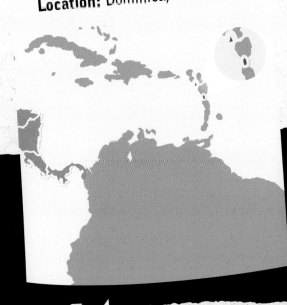

Rapid Response

When the disease struck Montserrat, conservationists immediately removed fifty healthy frogs. They were flown to zoos around the world, where they were kept in controlled rooms. Their keepers had to wear special clothes, masks, and gloves to make sure that no traces of the fungus got in from the outside world. Thanks to these measures, the frogs have bred well in captivity, and many have now been released back into the wild.

Wild Fact

A female mountain chicken lays thousands of **unfertilized** eggs to feed to her newly hatched tadpoles.

MEXICAN AXOLOTL

With its long tail and short legs, the axolotl is a species of salamander. Unlike its salamander cousins, the axolotl spends its whole life in water.

Axolotl Life

The Mexican axolotl is only found in the lakes and canals of Xochimilco near Mexico City, where it mostly stays on the muddy bottom. Young axolotl feed on **algae**. As they get older, their diet includes mollusks, worms, and **crustaceans**. This unusual amphibian breathes through feathery gills that branch out from the sides of its head.

Mexican axolotls are usually brown or black, but can be albino, like this captive axolotl.

Wild Fact

An axolotl finds its food by smell and by detecting electrical signals. It sucks its prey into its mouth and swallows it whole.

Struggling in the Wild

In the wild, axolotl numbers have fallen sharply. As Mexico City continues to grow, the axolotl's habitat is being drained to provide water to the city and is also badly polluted by chemicals and sewage. In 1998, there were an average of 6,000 axolotls per .4 square miles of canal water. Today, there are 35 per .4 square miles. The axolotl is now protected, and part of its habitat has been declared a national park.

A Mexican
axolotl larva
in captivity.

VITAL STATS

Scientific name:
Ambystoma mexicanum
Length: Up to 12 in.
Weight: Up to 6 oz.
Numbers in the wild: 700–1,200
Status: Critically endangered
Location: Mexico

Magical Powers

While the axolotl is struggling for survival in the wild, there are thousands in captivity, where they breed well. Some end up as pets. Others are studied by scientists because of the axolotl's amazing ability to regrow parts of its body. When an axolotl loses a limb, it can produce the tissue to grow a new one. Some axolotls go even further and grow another *extra* limb. Scientists hope that their findings can eventually help to treat wounds in humans.

Mexican axolotls have a
long fin that runs for most
of the length of their body.

MALLORCAN MIDWIFE TOAD

In 1980, groups of Mallorcan midwife toads were discovered in the Tramuntana Mountains in northern Mallorca, Spain. This was a thrilling find for scientists, as the toad was thought to have become extinct thousands of years ago.

A male Mallorcan midwife toad cares for his eggs until they hatch.

Model Males

Midwife toads get their name because of the care they show their young. In spring, the female lays a string of eggs that the male wraps around his back legs. When the eggs are ready to hatch, he wades into a stream and the tadpoles wriggle out. There is not much water in the toads' habitat, and this makes sure that the tadpoles have somewhere suitable to grow.

Wild Fact A Mallorcan midwife toad has a flattened body for squeezing under stones and into cracks in the rock, where it hides away from the hot sun and from predators.

Facing Danger

Since its rediscovery, numbers of Mallorcan midwife toads have fallen sharply. The toad faces many threats. Both adults and tadpoles are preyed on by snakes and frogs that have been brought to the island from elsewhere. The toads' vital water sources are dwindling, as the water is used to supply the growing numbers of tourists who visit the island on vacation. The toads have also been very badly affected by chytridiomycosis.

The toad's mottled brown coloring helps to camouflage it.

VITAL STATS

Scientific name: *Alytes muletensis*

Body Length:
Female: Up to 2 in.
Male: Up to 1.5 in.

Diet: Adults eat insects

Number in the wild:
Around 500 breeding pairs

Status: Vulnerable

Location: Mallorca, Spain

A scientist searches for the Mallorcan midwife toad in a mountain pond.

Saving the Toads

Over the past thirty years, conservationists have been working hard to increase the Mallorcan midwife toad's numbers. The toads breed well in captivity, and some captive-bred toads have been put back into the wild. One problem is that there are very few sites on the island that offer a suitable natural habitat for the toads, so new artificial breeding pools have been created just for them.

MONTSENY BROOK NEWT

The Montseny brook newt lives in cold mountain streams that run through Montseny Natural Park in Spain. A species of salamander, it has a dark-brown back, bright-yellow spots, and a cream-colored belly.

Holding on

Adapted to life in the water, the Montseny brook newt has a flattened head and body that allow it to slip into cracks in the rock. Scaly fingertips and skin help it cling to the bottom of streams, where it feeds on invertebrates. In spring and autumn, females lay their eggs in the stream.

A Montseny brook newt in northeastern Spain.

Flood and Drought

First discovered in 2005, numbers of these rare newts have dropped in the past ten years, and it is now one of the most endangered amphibians in Europe. The main threat that it faces is destruction of its natural habitat. Huge quantities of water from its mountain streams have been taken and sold as bottled water, leaving the streams dry. Heavy rains, on the other hand, can cause flash flooding, which can wash away whole communities of Montseny newts.

Saving the Salamander

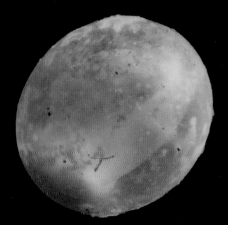

Now classed as critically endangered, the newt is protected by Spanish law. A conservation plan has been put into action to help manage water resources and protect the newt's habitat. A captive-breeding program was set up locally in 2007, and in 2010, 400 newts were released into the wild. Zoos in Spain and across Europe are now involved in helping this amphibian to survive.

These Montseny brook newt eggs are safely stored at a wildlife rehabilitation center in Spain.

VITAL STATS

Scientific name:
Calotriton arnoldi

Length: 3–4.5 in.

Diet: Aquatic invertebrates

Numbers in the wild:
Fewer than 1,500

Status: Critically endangered

Location: Spain

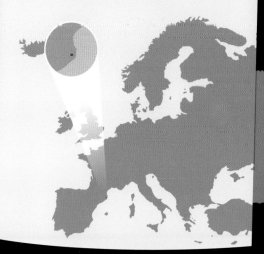

Wild Fact When a Montseny brook newt is threatened, it gives out a white, sticky, smelly substance from its skin to scare predators away.

SOUTHERN CORROBOREE FROG

The tiny southern corroboree frog from Australia has striking bright-yellow and black stripes. Its stunning appearance warns predators that the frog's skin is fatally poisonous and that they should stay away.

VITAL STATS

Scientific name:
Pseudophryne corroboree

Body Length: 1 in.

Diet: Ants, beetles, other invertebrates

Numbers in the wild:
Around 150

Status: Critically endangered

Location: Australia

Mountain Home

The southern corroboree frog lives only in the Snowy Mountains in New South Wales, Australia. It feeds and shelters in woodlands and heathland, under logs and rocks, and among **leaf litter**. In summer, the male frogs make nests of soft moss and grass near a bog or dried-up pool. They sing to attract females, who lay their eggs in the nests. The growing tadpoles remain inside the eggs until autumn, when the rains come and fill the pools with water. Once hatched, the tadpoles grow very slowly, especially over winter. They transform into adults the following summer when conditions are warmer.

Wild Fact Most frogs have webbed toes, but the southern corroboree frog does not, probably because it does not spend much time in water. It is also unusual in that it walks, rather than hops, from place to place.

Under Threat

The southern corroboree frog was once widespread, but, like many other species of frogs and toads, it has been hit hard by chytridiomycosis. Large numbers of tadpoles have also been killed by severe droughts that sometimes last for several years.

The frog's habitat in the Snowy Mountains, Australia.

A southern corroboree frog nestled among some moss.

Frog Force

The Australian government has joined forces with various organizations, including zoos and sanctuaries, to launch a National Recovery Plan for the southern corroboree frog. Hundreds of frogs and eggs bred at Taronga Zoo in Sydney and Zoos Victoria have been released back into their habitat in special disease-free enclosures. Zoo staff make regular trips to the park to monitor the new arrivals. An adopt-a-frog program is helping to fund this work.

WESTERN LEOPARD TOAD

True to its name, the large and beautifully marked western leopard toad has yellow skin with a pattern of brown blotches.

Wild Toads

In the wild, the western leopard toad is only found in a small area near the coast in the Western Cape province of South Africa. It lives around **wetlands**, lakes, and slow-moving rivers, where it forages for insects and other **invertebrates**. Its skin contains a powerful poison to protect it from predators such as snakes, birds, and fish.

The leopard toad gets its name from its leopard-like markings.

Roads and Toads

The spread of towns and cities into its wild habitat is putting the western leopard toad under threat. Not only is it losing its natural home, but, at the start of the rainy season, many toads are run over as they cross busy roads to reach their breeding pools. Others fall into steep-sided drains and swimming pools, from which they cannot escape. At their breeding pools, there are other dangers, including predators such as fish and ducks, which feed on the toads' eggs and tadpoles.

A road sign warns drivers to watch for leopard toads crossing the road.

Leopard Toad Crossing

Tracking the Toad

The western leopard toad is a protected species, but many toads are found outside the safety of the region's national parks and nature reserves. Several conservation organizations are working to save them. In urban areas, warning signs have been placed at key crossing places on busy roads, and volunteers are on hand to rescue the toads. People are also encouraged to make their gardens more toad-friendly by covering swimming pools.

A leopard toad foraging among river plants.

VITAL STATS

Scientific name: *Amietophrynus pantherinus*

Body length: Up to 6 in.

Diet: Insects, other invertebrates

Numbers in the wild: Unknown

Status: Endangered

Location: South Africa

Wild Fact The western leopard toad is also called the snoring toad because a male attracts a female by making a loud snoring call!

LEMUR LEAF FROG

During the day, a tiny lemur leaf frog is mostly greenish-yellow, making it well camouflaged as it rests on leaves. At night, its body changes to brown to blend in with the darkness.

Life on a Leaf

Lemur leaf frogs are only found in small patches of rain forest in Costa Rica, Panama, and Colombia. The lemur leaf frog is nocturnal. It hunts its prey of insects and other invertebrates at night, walking slowly through the branches and leaves. When day breaks, it finds a leaf to rest on and curls up underneath it.

Nursery Pool

During the rainy season, the male frog calls to attract a female for mating. She lays up to thirty eggs on top of a leaf that hangs over a pool of water. The tadpoles hatch about a week later and drop into the water or are washed in by the rain. It then takes another three to four months for the tadpoles to develop into adult frogs. The warmer the water, and the more food there is, the faster they grow.

A lemur leaf frog clinging to a rain forest plant.

VITAL STATS

Scientific name: *Agalychnis lemur*

Body length: Up to 2 in.

Diet: Insects, other invertebrates

Numbers in the wild: Unknown

Status: Critically endangered

Location: Central America

Deforestation and Disease

The number of lemur leaf frogs in the wild has fallen by half in the last fifteen years. Its rain forest home is being destroyed at an alarming rate for timber and to clear space for mining, farming, roads, and settlements. It is also under threat from chytridiomycosis. Since 2003, the Costa Rican Amphibian Research Center has worked with zoos in Britain, Sweden, and the United States. They breed healthy lemur leaf frogs and release them into the Guayacán Rainforest Reserve, where they are carefully monitored.

Wild Fact When the frogs are around a year old, they develop a pattern of spots and splotches. Each frog has a unique pattern, which scientists can use to tell the frogs apart.

SAGALLA CAECILIAN

Caecilian are unusual amphibians with no limbs and a long wormlike body. Around 200 species are known. Many are threatened by habitat loss. One of the most endangered is the very rare Sagalla caecilian. First described in 2005, it is found only in southeast Kenya.

The Sagalla caecilian uses both its lungs and its skin to breathe.

Built for Burrowing

Scientists still know very little about this rare amphibian. Much of their knowledge is based on studies of other very similar caecilians. Like other caecilians, scientists think that the Sagalla caecilian spends its life hidden under tree logs or in the soil. Its body is built for burrowing, with a round head for pushing through the soil. Its small eyes are completely covered in skin and bone, and it is practically blind. It uses smell to find its way around and locate its prey of termites and worms.

Shrinking Habitat

Caecilians must live in damp soil to supply them with food and keep their skin moist. This is important for breathing. Because of habitat loss, however, the Sagalla caecilian is only found today in one location: a small patch of forest in Sagalla Hills in Kenya (left). Much of its natural habitat has been cleared to make space for small farms, banana groves, and eucalyptus plantations, all of which suck moisture from the soil. The area is also colonized by invasive plants.

Better Together

Conservationists are working to find out more about the Sagalla caecilian. In Kenya, the Sagalla Caecilian Conservation Project is involving local people in safeguarding the caecilian, while still being able to farm their fields. Actions include helping to prevent soil erosion by replacing lost vegetation, including indigenous trees, to improve and increase the amount of habitat available for the caecilians to live in.

VITAL STATS

Scientific name: *Boulengerula niedeni*

Body length: Up to 12 in.

Diet: Worms and termites

Numbers in the wild: Unknown

Status: Endangered

Location: Kenya

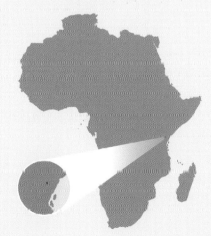

Wild Fact

For protection, a caecilian's smooth skin is toughened with **keratin**—the material that makes up our fingernails.

MALAGASY RAINBOW FROG

The Malagasy rainbow frog gets its name from the red, green, white, and black patterns on its back. It is found in Madagascar's Isalo Massif mountain range in steep-sided sandstone canyons, where it feeds on insects.

A Malagasy rainbow frog showing off its brilliant colors.

Rock Climber

Also known as the painted burrowing frog, this amazing amphibian is adapted for both digging and climbing. Underneath its back feet, it has large, hard growths that it uses like spades to scrape out a burrow in the sand. On its front feet, it has sticky discs for clinging to canyon walls and sharp claws on its fingers for gripping the rock. Being able to climb allows the frog to escape the flash floods that race through the canyons during the rainy season.

Life in the Gorge

The Malagasy rainbow frog lives mainly in an underground burrow to escape the heat and dry winds, but comes out to breed. The female lays her eggs in a temporary rock pool in the canyon. Here, the large, dark tadpoles grow into adults quickly, within one to two months, to avoid being washed away by floodwaters.

This Malagasy rainbow frog is seeking shade inside a succulent plant.

Too Beautiful

Because of its beautiful coloring, the Malagasy rainbow frog is highly valued as an exotic pet. Thousands of these frogs are trapped each year to supply the trade. Efforts are being made to limit and control this trade and to protect the frog in its shrinking wild habitat, which is under threat from tourism, wildfires, the cutting down of trees for firewood, livestock **overgrazing**, and mining for sapphires. Within the Isalo National Park, the frogs are protected, but they are very vulnerable outside the reserve.

VITAL STATS

Scientific name:
Scaphiophryne gottlebei
Body length: Up to 2 in.
Diet: Insects
Numbers in the wild: Unknown
Status: Endangered
Location: Madagascar

Wild Fact Unlike many frogs, the Malagasy rainbow frog is a poor swimmer, with short legs and webbing only on its back feet. This is probably because it spends more time on land than in water.

KIHANSI SPRAY TOAD

Unlike many amphibians, the Kihansi spray toad does not have a tadpole stage. The female toad gives birth to live toadlets, around .2 in. long. The skin on the female's belly is **translucent**, and the young can be seen growing inside.

Life in the Mist

The Kihansi spray toad is extremely rare and only found in a small patch of rocky wetland at the base of a waterfall called the Kihansi Falls in the Kihansi **Gorge**, Tanzania. The constant spray from the waterfall keeps conditions in its habitat cool and damp, and encourages thick moss and ferns to grow on the rocks.

A Kihansi spray toad in the wild.

Found and Lost

This tiny toad was only discovered in the late 1990s, when a healthy population of around 20,000 toads was recorded. By 2004, numbers had completely crashed, and only three toads were found in the wild. In the following years, no further toads were seen, and in 2009, the Kihansi spray toad was declared extinct in the wild. One of the main reasons for the toads' decline was the building of a **hydroelectric** dam close to the falls that opened in 2000. Around 90 percent of the water was diverted away from the falls and to the dam, drying up the toads' habitat.

A captive Kihansi spray toad at the Bronx Zoo, New York.

VITAL STATS

Scientific name: *Nectophrynoides asperginis*

Body length: Up to 1 in.

Diet: Insects and larvae

Numbers in the wild: More than 2,000

Status: Extinct in the wild

Location: Tanzania

To the Rescue

Luckily, scientists were prepared. In 2000, working with the government of Tanzania, two U.S. zoos removed nearly 500 toads from the wild for a captive-breeding program. The zoos built special enclosures for the toads that mimicked their wild habitat, and the program was a great success. In 2010, the first 100 toads were returned to the wild; in 2012, 2,000 toads were returned. Meanwhile, work had been carried out to repair the toad's habitat in Kihansi Gorge. An artificial misting system was set up that copied the original conditions of the waterfall.

Wild Fact Tiny flaps over the toad's nostrils prevent it from inhaling spray from its waterfall habitat.

QUITO ROCKET FROG

The Quito rocket frog is a small, mottled-brown frog that once thrived in tropical forests on the Andes Mountains in Ecuador and was even seen in the busy capital city of Quito. Today, it is only found in a small area in the shadow of the Cotopaxi volcano.

By the late 1980s, the Quito rocket frog was thought to be extinct.

Cool, Clear Water

The Quito rocket frog lives along cold mountain streams that flow into the Rio Pita River. The streams are fed with rain and melting snow and ice from Cotopaxi. In the 1980s, the frogs' numbers suddenly plummeted, most likely due to the spread of disease and habitat loss. In 1989, the last frog was recorded and scientists feared that it was on the verge of becoming extinct.

Eruption Danger

Astonishingly, in 2008, a group of Quito rocket frogs was discovered hidden under rocks on the banks of the Rio Pita. These were the last survivors of a whole species. The excitement over their discovery was short-lived, however. From August 2015 to January 2016, Cotopaxi began erupting, threatening to wipe the frogs out. Scientists launched an emergency rescue. Armed with flashlights and nets, they collected as many tadpoles as possible and removed them to safety at a local amphibian rescue organization, called Balsa de los Sapos (Life Raft for Frogs).

VITAL STATS

Scientific name:
Colostethus jacobuspetersi
Body length: 1 in.
Diet: Insects
Numbers in the wild: Unknown
Status: Critically endangered
Location: Ecuador

Wild Fact

As well as the Quito rocket frog, there are many different types of rocket frogs, including the striped rocket frog. They are named for their agile jumping abilities.

A Brighter Future

The Quito rocket frog is now part of a captive-breeding program at Balsa de los Sapos. Scientists study the frogs closely, trying to create exactly the right conditions for the frogs to breed. If this is successful, these frogs will be released in sites away from Cotopaxi. An adopt-a-tadpole program has been launched to help raise funds for this important work.

ENDANGERED

BIRDS

BIRDS IN DANGER

Today, one in six species of bird faces extinction, and it's largely due to human activity.

This chapter looks at some of the most endangered birds that face habitat loss, illegal hunting for meat, the pet trade, or poaching of their eggs.

WHAT ARE BIRDS?

- Vertebrates
- Warm-blooded
- Covered in feathers
- Hatch from eggs
- Have a beak, wings, and two legs

The Micronesian kingfisher is extinct in the wild. This captive bird lives in the Smithsonian National Zoo in Washington, D.C.

The famous dodo was a flightless bird that became extinct in the seventeenth century.

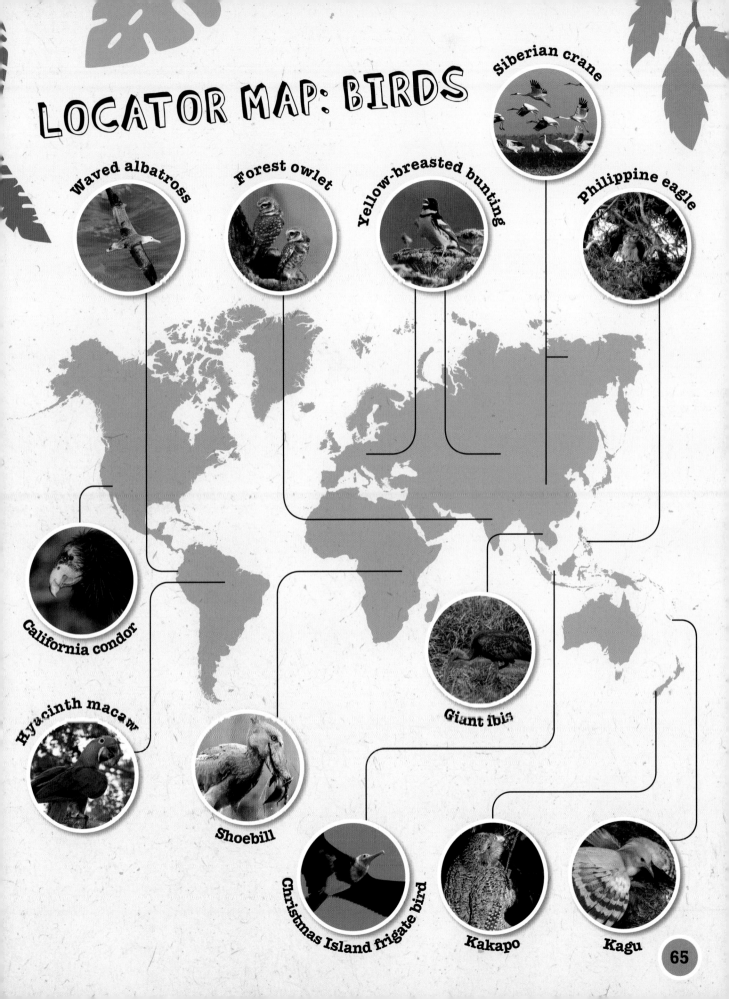

LOCATOR MAP: BIRDS

Siberian crane

Waved albatross

Forest owlet

Yellow-breasted bunting

Philippine eagle

California condor

Giant ibis

Hyacinth macaw

Shoebill

Christmas Island frigate bird

Kakapo

Kagu

GIANT IBIS

A large, striking bird, the giant ibis has a bald head and neck, dark-red eyes, and a long, curved bill. It lives in forests and around wetlands. The giant ibis mainly feeds on forest and wetland animals, such as locusts and cicadas, frogs, shellfish, and eels.

This giant ibis fell from its nest. A Cambodian woman from the local community nursed it back to health.

Shrinking Range

The giant ibis was once found over large parts of mainland Southeast Asia. Today, its range and numbers are shrinking fast. Most ibis live in Cambodia, with small numbers in Laos and possibly Vietnam. It is already extinct in Thailand and in danger everywhere else. Scientists estimate that, in total, there may be fewer than 250 giant ibis left in the wild.

The giant ibis lives alone or in small groups.

Under Threat

Across its range, the giant ibis is losing its habitat, as well as its breeding and feeding sites, causing a dramatic drop in its numbers. Forests are being cleared to make space for rubber and cassava plantations. Wetlands are being drained and turned into farmland. The ibis is also preyed upon by small mammals, such as yellow-throated martens and civets, and hunted by local people, who eat its meat and eggs.

Ibis Rescue

Measures are being taken to try to save the giant ibis. Conservationists have been tracking down ibis nesting sites in the forest. Then they fit smooth plastic belts around the base of the trees to stop predators from climbing up and stealing the ibis' eggs. They are also working closely with local people to protect the ibis' habitat. One project is for farmers to grow wildlife-friendly rice, known as ibis rice. The farmers agree only to farm in certain areas and not to use chemicals that might harm the birds' habitat. In return, the project buys the farmers' rice at a good price.

VITAL STATS

Scientific name:
Thaumatibis gigantea

Height: 3–3.5 ft.

Weight: 8–9.5 lbs.

Diet: Insects, eels, frogs, shellfish

Numbers in the wild:
Fewer than 250

Status: Critically endangered

Location: Southeast Asia

Wild Fact The giant ibis likes to forage for food in muddy water. It uses its long, curved bill to probe around in the mud for food, such as shellfish.

CALIFORNIA CONDOR

Soaring high above cliffs, the California condor spots the carcasses of dead animals by looking out for other scavengers, such as vultures. Then it swoops down, scaring the other birds away, and begins to feed. With a wingspan of almost 10 ft., it is the largest land bird in North America.

Giant Glider

The California condor has a bare, reddish-orange head and neck. Apart from two large white patches under its wings, its feathers are glossy black, with a black **ruff** around its neck. It can glide for several miles without flapping its gigantic wings, using rising **thermals** to help it stay in the air.

A California condor gliding with its huge wings.

Dying Out

California condors once lived across the western United States, close to cliffs or large trees that they use as nesting sites. By the beginning of the twentieth century, however, their numbers began to fall so dramatically that they could only be found in California. Over the last one hundred years, thousands have been killed by farmers to protect their cattle or poisoned by the lead from bullets used to kill the animals that the birds rely on for food. Another, more recent, threat comes from condors being killed by flying into overhead power lines.

This Californian condor chick was born in captivity.

VITAL STATS

Scientific name:
Gymnogyps californianus

Body length: 4–5 In.

Wingspan: 9–10 ft.

Weight: Around 20 lbs.

Diet: Dead animals

Number left in the wild:
Around 440

Status: Critically endangered

Location: Western U.S.

Back from the Brink

By 1987, there were only twenty-seven condors in the wild. To save the species, all the remaining birds were taken into a captive-breeding program. Four years later, some birds were successfully returned to the wild, and in 2003, the first wild condor chick in twenty years hatched. The condors are now closely monitored, and numbers are continuing to rise slowly but steadily.

Wild Fact To cool down, California condors urinate on their legs. This urine **evaporates** in the sun, drawing heat away from their bodies.

KAKAPO

The kakapo is a large, stocky parrot, found only in New Zealand. Unlike other parrots, the kakapo cannot fly. Instead, it runs through its forest home on its strong legs. It is also a good climber, using its powerful beak and claws to pull itself up into the trees. It comes out at night to look for food.

A kakapo feeds on supplejack berries.

Kakapo Crisis

Kakapos were once common in forests and grasslands all over New Zealand. Because they had no natural predators, they lost the ability to fly away. Unfortunately, the cats, rats, and stoats introduced by European settlers preyed on kakapos, driving them almost to extinction. Huge parts of the kakapos' habitat have also been cleared for farming, leaving only around 125 birds in the wild.

Safe Islands

To protect the remaining kakapos, the National Kakapo Team moved them to three predator-free islands off the coast of New Zealand. The birds are carefully monitored to make sure they are well fed and their chicks survive. Traps are also set to catch any predators that might swim over from the mainland.

This chick in a nest on Codfish Island is being monitored by a conservationist volunteer.

Slow Recovery

Thanks to the hard work of the conservationists, the number of kakapos has slowly increased from 51 in 1995 to around 125 today. Improvements in technology have also helped. Each kakapo is fitted with a radio transmitter that gives out a signal packed with information about the bird's behavior. By collecting this data, conservationists can track the kakapos and check them for signs of illness or injury. Sick or underweight chicks are also taken away and **hand-reared** before being returned to the wild.

VITAL STATS

Scientific name:
Strigops habroptila

Height at shoulder: 2 ft.

Weight: 4–9 lbs.

Diet: Fruit, leaves, roots, bark, seeds

Numbers in the wild: Approximately 125

Status: Critically endangered

Location: New Zealand

Wild Fact Although it cannot fly, a kakapo still has useful wings. It spreads them out to help it "parachute" down from a tree.

HYACINTH MACAW

With its bright-blue feathers and yellow-ringed eyes, the hyacinth macaw is a stunning bird. From its head to the tip of its tail, it can measure 3.5 ft. It uses its strong, curved beak to crack open nuts and seeds.

A hyacinth macaw in Brazil.

Macaw Life

The hyacinth macaw is found in only three places in South America, mainly in the Pantanal, a vast stretch of swampland in Brazil. It builds its nest in a cliff face or tree hole, which it makes bigger and fills with wood chips. The female lays one or two eggs inside, although usually only one chick survives.

Threats

Throughout its range, the hyacinth macaws' habitat has been destroyed to make space for farms, cattle ranches, and hydroelectric programs. Many macaws have also been killed by local people for their colorful feathers, which are used for decoration and art. The illegal pet trade is another major threat. In the 1980s, around 10,000 macaws were captured and sold as pets, fetching prices as high as $12,000. Despite an international ban, this trade continues today.

VITAL STATS

Scientific name: *Anodorhynchus hyacinthinus*
Body length: Up to 3.5 ft.
Weight: 2.5–4 lbs.
Diet: Nuts, seeds, fruits
Numbers in the wild: 6,500
Status: Endangered
Location: South America

Wild Fact

The hyacinth macaw has a dry, scaly tongue with a bone running along its length. The bone is used as a tool for opening nuts and fruits.

A pair of hyacinth macaws in a new nest box.

Action for Macaws

Launched in the 1980s, the Hyacinth Macaw Project in Brazil is dedicated to saving this beautiful bird. It works closely with local farmers to locate new nest sites. Conservationists capture the birds, weigh, measure, and band them, then put them back into the wild. A tree needs to be at least eighty years old to be strong enough to support a hyacinth macaw's nest, and there are fewer and fewer suitable sites available. The project has now developed light, artificial wooden nests, which can be fixed to younger trees, for the birds to use.

PHILIPPINE EAGLE

The world's largest and most powerful eagle, the Philippine eagle is only found on four islands in the Philippines, where it lives in dense mountain forests. It has dark-brown and cream feathers, with a shaggy feather crest around its head.

Eagle Hunter

A skilled hunter, the Philippine eagle feeds on flying lemurs and flying foxes, as well as snakes and lizards. It glides from perch to perch, working its way down through the trees before soaring back up again. Philippine eagles sometimes hunt in pairs to catch monkeys. One eagle acts as a **decoy** to distract the monkeys, while the other launches a surprise attack.

A Philippine eagle in its huge nest, high up in the trees.

Falling Numbers

Once widespread on the islands, there are now thought to be fewer than 250 Philippine eagles left in the wild. Their main threat is habitat loss, as the forests where they live are being cleared at an alarming rate for timber, farmland, and mining. The eagles have seen their habitat wiped out further by storms, floods, and mudslides, partly triggered by the massive deforestation. They are also shot by farmers trying to stop the eagles from attacking their livestock.

Saving the Eagle

The Philippine eagle is the national bird of the Philippines and is protected by law. Organizations, including the Philippine Eagle Foundation, monitor nests in the wild and run captive-breeding programs. They also train local people as "green guides" to protect nesting sites and prevent hunting. Despite their efforts, the eagles' population is unlikely to recover unless the loss of their habitat is stopped.

The Philippine eagle is the only bird of prey with blue eyes.

VITAL STATS

Scientific name: *Pithecophaga jefferyi*

Body length: 3 ft.

Wingspan: 7 ft.

Weight: 10–18 lbs.

Diet: Mainly monkeys, flying lemurs, lizards

Number left in wild: Fewer than 250

Status: Critically endangered

Location: Philippines

Wild Fact

A Philippine eagle's nest can measure 5 ft. across and is built in the crown of a tall tree. The nest looks like a platform of sticks and is lined with green leaves.

SIBERIAN CRANE

The Siberian crane is an elegant bird with white feathers and a red face and legs. Found in wetlands, it uses its long legs for wading and its long neck and bill for reaching underwater for plant roots to eat.

Winter Wanderer

The largest group of Siberian cranes breeds in eastern Russia in late spring. They build mound-shaped nests of reeds and grasses, surrounded by water. Inside, the female lays two eggs, which take about a month to hatch. In autumn, the cranes make a 3,110-mile journey to the Yangtze River in China.

Habitat Loss

The main threat facing the Siberian crane is loss of its habitat at its breeding and winter grounds, as well as at its **migration** stopovers. The cranes need a very specialized habitat, with plenty of shallow, fresh water. But people are draining wetlands for water for **irrigation** and to clear space for farming. The building of dams on the Yangtze River has also seriously affected the water level at the cranes' main winter grounds.

Siberian cranes preen their feathers to keep them clean and healthy.

Wetland Project

In 2003, the ICF (International Crane Foundation) launched the Siberian Crane Wetland Project. Working with governments and conservation organizations, its main aim was to protect vital "flyways"—the network of wetland sites on the cranes' migration routes. Many of these sites are now better protected, with plans in place to manage water levels, as well as the supply of water plants for the cranes to feed on during their journey. Further work is needed to protect their breeding and winter grounds.

A Siberian crane chick at a nature reserve in Russia.

A flock of Siberian cranes takes to the air.

VITAL STATS

Scientific name:
Leucogeranus leucogeranus

Height: Around 5 ft.

Weight: Around 13 lbs.

Diet: Mainly water plants; also fish, frogs, insects

Numbers in the wild: 3,500–4,000

Status: Critically endangered

Location: Russia/China

Wild Fact The Siberian crane has an unusual **serrated** bill for feeling for and gripping slippery plant roots in shallow water.

WAVED ALBATROSS

The waved albatross is a large seabird with a wingspan of more than 7 ft. It spends most of its life soaring above the ocean, searching for fish and squid to eat. It scoops its prey from the surface of the sea, often foraging near fishing boats.

A waved albatross soars above the Pacific Ocean.

A waved albatross with its chick.

Nursery Time

The waved albatross comes ashore to breed, mainly on Española Island in the Galápagos Islands. The female lays an egg on the bare ground, then the parents take turns **incubating** it for up to two months. A few weeks after hatching, the chick is left in "nursery" groups with other chicks, so the parents can go fishing. When the parents return, they **regurgitate** an oily, fishy liquid for the chicks to feed on.

Fatal Fishing

Although there are around 50,000 waved albatrosses, their numbers are falling fast. The biggest threat comes from long-line fishing boats off the coast of Peru, where the birds feed. These boats pull hundreds of miles of fishing line behind them, complete with baited hooks. Attracted by the bait, the birds swoop down, swallow the hooks, and are dragged under and drowned.

Scientists attach a satellite tracking device to a waved albatross.

VITAL STATS

Scientific name: *Phoebastria irrorata*

Body length: 3 ft.

Wingspan: 7.5–8 ft.

Weight: 7–9 lbs.

Diet: Fish, squid

Numbers in the wild: 50,000–70,000

Status: Critically endangered

Location: South America

Protected Places

Española is part of the Galápagos Marine Reserve, where long-line fishing is banned. Outside the reserve, though, it still goes on. Conservationists are working with fishing crews to find ways of reducing the danger to the albatrosses, while safeguarding the crews' livelihoods. These include using bird-scaring devices and fitting weights so that the lines sink more quickly.

Wild Fact

Apart from catching its own food, the waved albatross also steals food from other birds, chasing them until they are forced to regurgitate their catch.

CHRISTMAS ISLAND FRIGATE BIRD

A Christmas Island frigate bird can stay in the air for more than a week at a time. It feeds on fish and squid, swooping down to pluck them from the surface.

A majestic Christmas Island frigate bird in flight.

Island Nests

The frigate bird spends most of its time at sea, but comes ashore to breed on Christmas Island in the Indian Ocean. Colonies of birds build their nests in trees along the shore, with up to twenty nests in one tree. The female lays a single egg once every two years.

Wild Fact Male Christmas Island frigate birds have a red pouch on their throats that they use to attract females at breeding time. A male inflates his pouch like a balloon, tips his head back, and drums on it with his beak.

Dust and Ants

With only around 4,000 adults in the wild, and such a slow breeding rate, the Christmas Island frigate bird is at serious risk. About a quarter of the island's forests and, with them, the frigate birds' nesting sites, have been cleared for phosphate mining. Nesting sites are also being polluted by dust from the phosphate and destroyed by yellow crazy ants that feed on—and kill—the trees.

Two Christmas Island frigate birds enjoy playing in flight.

VITAL STATS

Scientific name: *Fregata andrewsi*
Body length: Up to 3.5 ft.
Wingspan: Up to 7.5 ft.
Weight: 3–4 lbs.
Diet: Fish, squid, seabird eggs, and chicks
Number left in the wild: Around 4,000
Status: Critically endangered
Location: Christmas Island, Australia

Recovery Plan

In 1989, the Christmas Island National Park was set up to help protect the birds. Most of their nesting sites lie inside the park and are closely monitored. Other conservation actions include treating the ants with **insecticide** and installing equipment to keep the amount of phosphate dust down. In 2004, a National Recovery Plan was also launched but did not have much success. Another plan is being developed to include all of the island's unique wildlife.

Christmas Island is home to many rare creatures.

SHOEBILL

The extraordinary-looking shoebill is a stork-like bird from Africa, with blue-green feathers and long legs for wading in water. Its most famous feature is its huge, shoe-shaped bill, which ends in a deadly hook.

Swamp Stalker

The shoebill lives in freshwater swamps and marshes with plenty of dense papyrus grass and reeds. It usually feeds on large fish, such as lungfish, but will also eat water snakes, amphibians, and waterbird chicks. It stalks its prey by walking very slowly or standing completely still. When prey is spotted, it strikes with great speed and power, grabbing its victim with its fearsome bill.

A shoebill catches a slimy lungfish.

A two-month-old shoebill stands in its nest.

Nest Building

Shoebills usually live alone, except at breeding time. Then both parents build a large nest from water plants on a floating platform among the reeds. Inside, the female lays up to three white eggs, which both parents incubate in turn. The chicks hatch after about thirty days and are fed by their parents until they start hunting for themselves at around three to four months old.

Wild Fact

A shoebill has very big feet, with its middle toes reaching 7 in. long. This helps it to stand and balance on floating water plants while it hunts.

VITAL STATS

Scientific name: *Balaeniceps rex*

Height: 4–5 ft.

Weight: 9–15 lbs.

Diet: Fish, amphibians, chicks, snakes

Number left in wild: 5,000–8,000

Status: Vulnerable

Location: Eastern Africa

Losing Habitat

Although the shoebill is found across eastern Africa, there are only a few thousand left in the wild. Their numbers are falling because of hunting, capture for the pet trade, and destruction of their wetland habitat. Wetlands provide a valuable home for wildlife, as well as water supplies and farmland for local people. Conservationists are working to encourage local people to protect the wetlands and to find new ways of making a living, including acting as tourist guides, selling handicrafts, and bee-keeping.

KAGU

The kagu lives on Grande Terre, the largest island of New Caledonia, in the South Pacific Ocean. Local people call it the "ghost of the forest" because of its striking pale-gray feathers. The kagu has a bright-orange bill and legs, and a crest of feathers on its head.

Ground-floor Living

Kagus live on the forest floor, where they forage for insects, spiders, and millipedes among the leaf litter. They often stand still, on one foot, waiting patiently, then strike and catch prey in their long, pointed bills. They look for food during the day and sleep at night on low branches, tree trunks, or rocks on the ground.

A kagu chick begins life with dark-brown feathers before it grows its gray plumage.

Wing Warning

Although it has large wings, a kagu hardly ever flies. To escape from danger, it runs away on its long legs. Its wings are still important, though. If a predator threatens a kagu chick, the parent opens its wings and flaps them on the ground, which startles the predator. Kagus also use their wings for balance as they walk and run.

A kagu with its wings spread out as a warning.

Kagu Crisis

Over the last 200 years, kagu numbers have dropped dramatically. One of the greatest threats comes from predators, such as dogs, cats, and rats brought to the island by settlers. Kagus were also hunted for meat and for their crest feathers, which were used for making hats, while their forest home has been cleared for mining and timber. The kagu is now protected by law. Captive-bred kagus have been successfully put back in the wild in a national park where predators are carefully monitored.

VITAL STATS

Scientific name:
Rhynochetos jubatus

Body length: Around 2 ft.

Wingspan: Around 3 ft.

Weight: 1.5–2.5 lbs.

Diet: Insects, spiders, millipedes

Number left in the wild:
Fewer than 2,000

Status: Critically endangered

Location: New Caledonia

Kagus are hunted for their ghostly white feathers.

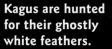

Wild Fact Kagus have special feathers, called powder downs. The tips of these feathers disintegrate, forming a dustlike powder that keeps the kagus' feathers clean, dry, and in good condition.

YELLOW-BREASTED BUNTING

The yellow-breasted bunting was once common across Europe and Asia, its range stretching from Finland to Japan. But in the last twenty to thirty years, its numbers have plummeted by as much as 90 percent. Today, there may be as few as 60,000 left.

Rice Birds

On its migration, the bunting passes through eastern China. Here, it is known as the rice bird and has been hunted for food for hundreds of years. The birds are caught in nets at their stopover sites in rice-paddy fields, where they gather in large flocks at night, making them an easy target. Hunting them has been banned in China since 1997, but tens of thousands of buntings are still killed and sold illegally, pushing them toward extinction at an alarming rate.

A yellow-breasted bunting looks after its six chicks.

Bunting Life

The bunting breeds in northeast Europe and northern Asia. It lays four to six eggs in a nest on scrubland, often near water. It then travels east with its young to spend the winter in warmer Southeast Asia.

A male yellow-breasted bunting sings to attract a mate.

Urgent Action

BirdLife International is putting together a plan to save the yellow-breasted bunting, but various actions are already being taken. In Russia, a group of birds has had color-coded bands fitted around their legs so that they can be tracked and protected on their migration and at their breeding sites. In China, eating buntings is now illegal, and posters have been produced to make people more aware of the birds' plight.

VITAL STATS

Scientific name: *Emberiza aureola*

Body length: 6 in.

Weight: 1 oz.

Diet: Insects, seeds

Numbers in the wild: 60,000–300,000

Status: Critically endangered

Location: Europe, Asia

Wild Fact Yellow breasted buntings eat seeds, but feed insects to their young.

FOREST OWLET

A small, stocky owl with a large head and huge yellow eyes, the forest owlet lives in forests in central India. Unlike other owls, it is active during the day, when it hunts for food.

Two forest owlets at a national reserve in India.

Back to Life

Experts thought that the forest owlet was already extinct when it was rediscovered in a forest in central India in 1997, more than one hundred years after a sighting had last been recorded. Three years later, more birds were located at four new sites, and sightings are still being made. More than one hundred owlets have been found in the Melghat Tiger Reserve, a protected national park.

Owl Prey

The forest owlet feeds on small animals found among the trees, such as lizards, small birds, rodents, and insects. It sits still on a perch and waits for its prey, then it swoops down and strikes with its talons. It often stores prey in hollow tree trunks.

A forest owlet is well camouflaged in the leaves of a teak tree.

Under Pressure

The remaining owlets survive only in small patches of forest, and these patches are in danger of being cleared for timber and firewood collection, and to make space for farmland. The owls are also killed by local people because they are thought to be unlucky. Hunting and trapping the owls is now banned by the Indian government, but more needs to be done to protect the birds' nesting sites and habitat.

VITAL STATS

Scientific name:
Heteroglaux blewitti

Body length: Around 9 in.

Weight: Unknown

Diet: Lizards, birds, insects

Number left in wild:
Fewer than 250

Status: Critically endangered

Location: Central India

Wild Fact A forest owlet's talons are so large that it can catch prey up to twice its own size.

ENDANGERED
INSECTS AND
INVERTEBRATES

INSECTS AND OTHER INVERTEBRATES IN DANGER

Today, animals facing extinction include hundreds of species of insects and other invertebrates. An uncertain future for these creatures means an uncertain future for many plants on Earth too. For example, bees feed on the nectar from flowering plants, helping to **pollinate** them so that the plants can produce seeds and new plants. Without the bees, the plants would die out.

WHAT ARE INVERTEBRATES?

- Don't have a backbone
- Some, such as worms, have soft bodies
- Some, such as insects, have a hard outer body, called an exoskeleton

The large blue butterfly was brought back from extinction in the U.K. through a reintroduction program.

LOCATOR MAP:
INSECTS AND INVERTEBRATES

Peacock tarantula

American burying beetle

Ladybird spider

Epirus dancing grasshopper

Sinai baton blue

Franklin's bumblebee

Seychelles giant millipede

Cederberg cave katydid

Queen Alexandra's birdwing butterfly

Lord Howe Island stick insect

Dracula ant

Basking malachite

LORD HOWE ISLAND STICK INSECT

The Lord Howe Island stick insect is a dark-brown, wingless insect that can grow up to 5 in. long. Only found on the remote Lord Howe Island, 370 miles off the east coast of Australia, it was thought to be extinct.

Raging Rodents

The Lord Howe Island stick insect once lived in abundance on this isolated island. However, in 1918, a ship ran aground on the island. The ship had hundreds of black rats on board that quickly invaded Lord Howe Island. The rats fed on the island's birds and insects, including the Lord Howe Island stick insect, and its numbers plummeted. In 1983, it was officially declared extinct.

The Lord Howe Island stick insect has no wings, but it is able to run quickly on its sturdy legs.

Wild Fact

The female Lord Howe Island stick insect lays her eggs in soil and then buries them. She can lay up to 300 eggs in her lifetime.

The tiny volcanic island of Ball's Pyramid.

An Amazing Discovery

In 2001, scientists found a small colony of stick insects on a tiny nearby island, called Ball's Pyramid. They had been feeding from the leaf tips of tea-tree shrubs. The stick insects had survived on this remote island because it is rat-free. The scientists collected several pairs and transported them to Melbourne Zoo, where a successful captive breeding program was begun.

A Lord Howe stick insect at Melbourne Zoo, Australia.

VITAL STATS

Scientific name: *Dryococelus australis*

Body length: Up to 5 in.

Diet: Tea-tree shrubs

Numbers in the wild: 20–40

Status: Critically endangered

Location: Australia

A Surprising Find

Scientists at Melbourne Zoo did not realize that the stick insects found on Ball's Pyramid were from the same species as Lord Howe Island stick insects, which they knew about from museum specimens. DNA testing, however, has proven that the two groups of insects do indeed belong to the same species. There are now 9,000 in captivity in Australia, Canada, and the U.K. The plan is to rid Lord Howe Island of black rats and mice, and reintroduce the stick insects there.

QUEEN ALEXANDRA'S BIRDWING BUTTERFLY

With a huge wingspan of up to 11 in., the Queen Alexandra's birdwing is the largest butterfly in the world. The males shimmer with bright blue-green patterns, while the females' wings are dark with yellow-and-white markings.

In the Pipevine

The Queen Alexandra's birdwing lives only in small patches of rain forest in eastern Papua New Guinea. Adults feed and breed on plants called pipevines that wind their way up the trunks of rain forest trees. The female lays her eggs on the underside of a pipevine leaf, which provides a food source when the caterpillars hatch. The leaves are poisonous but do not harm the caterpillars. Instead, the caterpillars digest the poison, making them toxic to predators.

The female Queen Alexandra's birdwing butterfly is larger than the male.

A male Queen Alexandra's birdwing's wingspan is smaller than the female's, at around 8 in.

Under Threat

For many years, the Queen Alexandra's birdwing has been under threat from collectors, who can earn thousands of dollars for each butterfly. It is now protected by law, but some butterflies are still collected illegally. The greatest danger that they face, however, is the destruction of their rain forest habitat, which is being cleared for logging and farming, particularly of palm oil.

Birdwing Rescue

Conservation action is urgently needed to save the Queen Alexandra's birdwing. In 2017, a new project was launched in Papua New Guinea. The aim was to involve the palm oil industry in working with conservationists to protect the butterflies. A laboratory is being built where the butterflies can be safely bred in captivity, and nurseries are being set up where supplies of pipevine plants can be grown.

VITAL STATS

Scientific name:
Ornithoptera alexandrae
Wingspan: Up to 11 in. (female)
Up to 8 in. (male)
Diet: Pipevine leaves and flowers
Numbers in the wild: Unknown
Status: Endangered
Location:
Papua New Guinea

Wild Fact

Queen Alexandra's birdwing caterpillars have dark-red bodies, with bright red-and-yellow spines. This warns predators that they are poisonous to eat.

LADYBIRD SPIDER

This spider gets its name from the male's red, velvety **abdomen** with its black spots. A male's colors appear when it is ready to breed. Until then, like the female, its body is black.

A Deadly Nest

The ladybird spider lives among European heathlands, where it builds its burrow. The burrow is lined with silk and is surrounded by silk threads. These act like trip wires for catching insect prey and help the spider catch victims much bigger than itself, including the violet ground beetle, which is twice its size. When the male is ready to breed, it goes in search of a female. At her burrow, he plucks the trip wires in a special way so she knows he is not prey.

Wild Fact

After mating in May, a female spider lays over fifty eggs in a silk cocoon inside her burrow. The spiderlings hatch in July or August.

A female ladybird spider guards her tunnellike underground burrow.

A male ladybird spider shows off its bright-red spotted abdomen.

Heather Habitat

Once found across northern and central Europe, the ladybird spider is now very rare. In the U.K., it only survives on a few patches of heathland in Dorset. A group of spiders was discovered there in 1980, after the spider was thought to be extinct in the U.K. Loss of its natural habitat is the main reason for the spider's decline. Large areas of heathland have been cleared for farming or taken over by other shrubs that do not naturally grow there.

Conservationists take photos of the ladybird spider.

VITAL STATS

Scientific name:
Eresus sandaliatus

Length: .4–.6 in.

Diet: Insects

Numbers in the wild:
Around 1,000 (U.K.)

Status: Endangered

Location: U.K. and Europe

Saving Spiders

By the 1990s, the number of ladybird spiders in the U.K. had fallen to just fifty. A conservation agency began a recovery program to clear their Dorset habitat of shrubs that do not naturally grow there and to find suitable burrowing sites. This has been so successful that spider numbers have reached almost 1,000. In 2017, the Back from the Brink Project was launched to monitor the spiders and establish more sites. The spiders are taken to their new homes in plastic bottles filled with leaf litter. The bottles are then planted in the ground in the wild, giving the spiders a ready-made home.

DRACULA ANT

The Dracula ant has a gruesome habit: it drinks the blood of its young! This unusual insect lives in colonies among leaf litter and rotting logs in Madagascar.

Family Life

Worker Dracula ants are light orange in color, winged males are dark orange, and the queens are yellow. Dracula ant larvae are white. Every day, the workers go out into the forest to hunt for food, stunning their prey of smaller insects with venom before bringing them back to the colony for the larvae to feed on. Worker ants and queens do not eat this prey themselves. Instead, they chew holes in the larvae's bodies and suck out a yellow-green liquid, called hemolymph, which is like the ants' blood. Amazingly, the larvae survive.

A dracula ant biting the skin of a larva to sip its haemolymph.

Dracula in Danger

Dracula ants only live in a small patch of dry, tropical forest in Madagascar on a high plateau close to the island's capital, Antananarivo. The main threat to their survival is the loss of their forest habitat, as the city grows and trees are cut down to make space for farming.

Ant Academy

The species was only discovered in 1994, when twenty-one Dracula ants were found on the surface of a rotten log. In 2001, Dr. Brian Fisher of the California Academy of Sciences discovered a whole colony. Since then, Fisher has studied the ants closely, moving several colonies into his laboratory as a safeguard against the species becoming extinct. Fisher has also discovered another species of Dracula ant, this one with long, snapping jaws.

VITAL STATS

Scientific name:
Adetomyrma venatrix

Body length:
Worker ant—about 1 in.

Diet: Dracula ant larvae hemolymph

Numbers in the wild: Unknown

Status: Critically endangered

Location: Madagascar

Wild Fact A colony of Dracula ants may contain up to 10,000 workers, together with winged males and several wingless queens.

SEYCHELLES GIANT MILLIPEDE

Found only on fourteen small islands in the Seychelles in the Indian Ocean, this sleek giant millipede can grow up to 12 in. long.

Life in the Leaf Litter

The millipede lives in tropical forests, where it crawls along the ground and sometimes ventures up trees. It avoids the daytime heat by burrowing into leaf litter or soil. It feeds mostly on leaf litter and fallen fruit, helping to break them down, and then **excretes** plant waste back into the soil. This makes the soil deeper and richer so that forest trees and plants can thrive.

A Seychelles giant millipede in its forest habitat.

Isolated Island

The largest surviving population of giant millipedes lives on the Seychelles island of Cousine. On other islands, their habitat has been taken over by non-native plants, such as bamboo and coconut, introduced by settlers, and the millipedes are preyed on by introduced animals, such as rats. On Cousine there are no predators, and steps have been taken to protect the millipedes' habitat by planting more native trees.

A Seychelles giant millipede, compared to a human hand.

Millipede Rescue

To safeguard the millipede, a captive-breeding program was started at London Zoo. In 2006, the zoo sent twelve adult millipedes to an agricultural college in Cornwall, England, to start its own breeding program. The millipedes are kept at a warm temperature in a large glass tank filled with a deep layer of **peat** that is mixed with oak leaves and rotten wood. Every day, staff spray the millipedes with a mist of water. So far, their efforts have been rewarded, with more than 200 young born in the first two years.

VITAL STATS

Scientific name:
Seychelleptus seychellarum

Body length: Up to 12 in.

Diet: Rotten leaves, fruit

Numbers in the wild:
Around 750,000

Status: Endangered

Location: Seychelles

Wild Fact To protect itself from predators, the Seychelles giant millipede produces a brown liquid, which can be poisonous, from glands in its skin.

FRANKLIN'S BUMBLEBEE

The critically endangered Franklin's bumblebee is only known to live in a small mountainous area in Southern Oregon and Northern California. However, it has not been seen since 2006, and scientists fear that it might already be extinct.

A Franklin's bumblebee feeding on flower nectar.

Feast of Flowers

A Franklin's bumblebee has a black body, with a broad U-shaped patch of yellow on its head. It feeds on nectar and pollen from a range of wildflowers, including California poppies, lupines, and vetch. The Franklin's bumblebee is vitally important for pollination so that seeds and new plants can grow.

Busy Bees

Like other bumblebees, Franklin's bumblebees live in colonies of a queen, workers, and males. They are thought to nest among clumps of grass or in unused rodent burrows. In spring, the queen lays her eggs and feeds on nectar until the larvae hatch and build their cocoons. Worker bees emerge first to feed the queen. Males and queens hatch later, when the old queen's job is complete and she has died.

Wild Fact

As the Franklin's bumblebee feeds, it vibrates inside the flower, scattering pollen across its back and carrying it to other flowers.

A Rapid Decline

In the 1990s, Franklin bumblebees were seen fairly often. But their numbers have fallen rapidly, and since a single bee was spotted in 2006, no others have been seen. Some conservationists in the United States think that **herbicides**, **pesticides**, or a deadly fungal disease could be among the causes. The bees' limited habitat has been damaged by farming, house and road building, as well as forest fires. Conservationists are still searching for the Franklin's bumblebee across its range.

The body of this Franklin's bumblebee is on exhibit at the Smithsonian Museum of Natural History in Washington, D.C.

VITAL STATS

Scientific name: *Bombus franklini*

Body length: Unknown

Diet: Flower pollen and nectar

Numbers in the wild: Unknown

Status: Critically endangered

Location: Southern Oregon to Northern California

BASKING MALACHITE

The basking malachite is a striking damselfly, with a bright metallic-green body and lacelike wings. It is found in only two locations in South Africa's Eastern Cape, along the Kubusi and Thorn Rivers.

Sun Basking

This dazzling insect lives by clear, rocky streams, with plenty of long grass and overhanging bushes along the banks. It can often be seen perched on a plant, with its wings open, basking in the sun, or snapping up insects from the water. Females use the riverbank plants for laying their eggs. When the larvae hatch, they drop into the water, where they feed on small invertebrates, such as mosquitoes and midges.

A male basking malachite, perched on a plant.

A Fragile Habitat

In the 1970s, the basking malachite was found in at least ten sites. By 2001, this had fallen to two. The main problem is that their habitat is located among farmland grazed by livestock, such as cattle. The cattle trample the riverbank plants, destroying the malachites' egg-laying sites. Another threat comes from the rapid growth of the non-native tree called black wattle, which blocks sunlight from reaching the river. This means that water plants cannot grow, affecting the insects that feed on them, which the damselflies eat.

The growth of black wattle has had an impact on the basking malachite's feeding sites.

Working for Water

So far, very little conservation work has been carried out on behalf of the basking malachite, and its habitat is not yet protected. Launched in 1995, the South African organization Working for Water has started to cut back the black wattle trees to save the damselflies' habitat. Some farmers have also agreed to monitor their cattle's movements, allowing them only to enter streams at certain points.

VITAL STATS

Scientific name:
Chlorolestes apricans
Body length: Up to 1.5 in.
Wingspan: Up to 2 in.
Diet: Insects
Numbers in the wild:
Fewer than 1,000
Status: Endangered
Location: South Africa

Wild Fact Like other damselflies, the basking malachite has huge compound eyes and sharp eyesight for spotting and catching its prey in midair.

PEACOCK TARANTULA

With its colorful body, striped legs, and patterned abdomen, the peacock tarantula is one of the world's most dazzling spiders. It lives in deciduous forests in Andhra Pradesh, central India.

Tree House Life

In the wild, peacock tarantulas live in tall forest trees. They build their funnel-shaped webs in holes in the tree trunks. They hunt at night, locating their prey of insects with limb-like feelers, which can sense movement and smells.

The peacock tarantula is also known as a gooty sapphire ornamental tree spider.

Peacock Colors

The peacock tarantula gets its name from its brilliant colors. Its body is covered in bright-blue hairs, even on the underside of its eight legs. The coloring comes from tiny crystals on the hairs that reflect blue light. Scientists are still unsure what the spider uses its colors for. It may be for attracting a mate or to help it blend in with the forest shadows, hiding it from predators such as birds, as well as its prey of insects. A young peacock spider has a brown body. It gets its blue coloring as it grows up.

A peacock tarantula shows its bright-blue and yellow legs.

No Hiding Place

This very rare spider had not been seen for more than one hundred years until it was spotted in 2001. Today, it is only found in a single small patch of forest inside a **wildlife sanctuary**. However, the trees it relies on for its home and food are being cut down illegally for timber and firewood and to clear the land for farming. Peacock tarantulas are also sold as exotic pets. Experts are studying the tarantulas, but much more work needs to be done to protect them.

VITAL STATS

Scientific name:
Poecilotheria metallica

Leg span: Up to 8 in.

Diet: Insects, such as crickets

Numbers in the wild: Unknown

Status: Critically endangered

Location: India

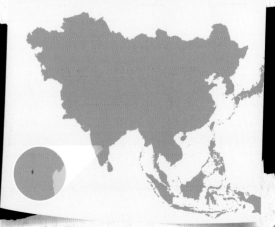

Wild Fact If the peacock tarantula is threatened, it will usually run away very fast, but it has a venomous bite if it needs to defend itself.

EPIRUS DANCING GRASSHOPPER

Only found in Epirus, in the northwest of mainland Greece, the Epirus dancing grasshopper lives in several groups around three lakes. It clings to tall wetland plants— camouflaged by its beige color.

An Epirus dancing grasshopper in Paramithia, Greece.

Great Movers

The dancing grasshopper gets its name from the intricate, ballet-like dance that the males do to attract females for mating. After mating, in late summer the females lay their eggs, which spend the winter lying **dormant** under the lakes' chilly waters. In June, the young emerge and feed greedily until they reach adulthood. By August, they are mature enough to mate.

Flood and Feast

The grasshoppers live on wet grasslands, which flood every winter. Rains flood the lakeshores, forming bogs and marshlands with rich soil—the perfect conditions for wetland plants to grow. Scientists have found the biggest populations of grasshopper in places where there is the greatest variety of plants.

The Epirus dancing grasshopper can be found in wetland areas around the Pamvotida Lake basin.

VITAL STATS

Scientific name: *Chorthippus lacustris*

Body length: Unknown

Diet: Wetland plants

Numbers in the wild: Unknown

Status: Critically endangered

Location: Greece

Clinging On

Scientists only discovered the Epirus dancing grasshopper in 1975. In the last forty years or so, it has lost around 90 percent of its habitat. Its wetland home has been drained to create new land for farming and building, which has meant its numbers have decreased dramatically. Today, the grasshoppers' remaining habitat totals just 5 square miles, split into smaller sites. These belong to the Natura 2000 conservation network, but urgent work is needed to restore the wetlands and monitor the grasshoppers.

Wild Fact As with all grasshoppers, the Epirus dancing grasshopper has its eardrums on each side of its abdomen, under its wings.

CEDERBERG CAVE KATYDID

Katydids are insects that are related to crickets. They are found all over the world, mostly in tropical regions, where they live on bushes and trees. One species from South Africa has a more unusual home. It lives in a few dark caves in the Cederberg Mountains.

Cave Life

The only known cave-dwelling katydid, this extraordinary insect is well adapted to its narrow dark home deep in the sandstone. It uses its 6-in.-long **antennae** to help it feel its way in the dark and locate other katydids. Its feet are extremely sticky, so it can walk upside down on the cave ceiling. In the dark, there is no point having bright colors, so its body is pale.

Cederberg cave katydids blend in well with the mountains' rich sandstone.

Chilly Home

The katydids prefer caves that are a chilly 54°F all year round. This is perfect for the katydids, but more importantly, it is also too cold to worry about sharing their space with cave-dwelling would-be predators, such as **hyraxes** and bats. However, there is almost nothing for the katydids to eat in the cave, so they must leave their chilly homes at night and forage for grasses and other plants near the cave mouth.

The Cederberg caves in South Africa, where the katydid lives.

A Fragile Future

The main threat to this unique species is climate change, which is already causing southern Africa to warm up. This could raise the temperature in the caves and encourage the katydids' predators inside. Luckily, the caves lie within the Cederberg Wilderness Protected Area and their habitat is monitored for other threats, such as tourism. **Entomologists** also visit the caves to study the insects and have recently discovered a small, new katydid cave that they did not know of before.

VITAL STATS

Scientific name:
Cedarbergeniana imperfecta
Length: Up to 2.5 in.
Diet: Grasses, other plants
Numbers in the wild: Unknown
Status: Critically endangered
Location: South Africa

Wild Fact Katydids are normally solitary, but this species is sociable. It is often found in groups with twenty to thirty others.

SINAI BATON BLUE

One of the world's smallest butterflies, the Sinai baton blue is no bigger than a thumbnail. Male butterflies have bright-blue wings, edged with black and white, while females are dark brown.

Precious Plants

This delicate insect is found on a mountainside in southern Sinai in Egypt, where they feed only on nectar from Sinai thyme plants' small flowers. But this little bush provides more than simply food—it is crucial for the butterfly's life cycle.

In spring, the female lays around twenty-five tiny eggs on a thyme flower. After a few days, the eggs hatch and green caterpillars crawl out. They feed on the thyme flowers and grow, before dropping to the ground. Here, they form **pupae** that stay in the soil over winter and turn into adults the following May, as the thyme flowers bloom.

Restricted Range

The precious thyme plant that the Sinai baton blue depends on only grows in a tiny area of the Sinai mountainside. But the thyme bushes are being wiped out by droughts, high winds, the effects of climate change, and humans who pick the leaves and flowers for cooking. If the thyme disappears, the Sinai baton blue will not be able to survive.

A male Sinai baton blue butterfly feeds on the nectar of a wild thyme plant.

A female Sinai baton blue butterfly.

Saving Thyme

To save the butterflies, conservationists must first protect the thyme plants. Picking the thyme is now banned. A fence has been built around the largest patch of thyme to stop people from trampling on the plants, and two dams have been constructed to make sure that the thyme is well watered. Rangers monitor the butterflies and their habitat, and run educational programs to involve local people in the butterflies' care.

VITAL STATS

Scientific name:
Pseudophilotes sinaicus

Wingspan: Around .4 in.

Diet: Thyme plants

Numbers in the wild:
Around 2,000

Status: Critically endangered

Location: Egypt

Wild Fact The Sinai baton blue caterpillar allows ants to protect and clean it. In return, the caterpillar oozes a sugary syrup for the ants to feed on.

AMERICAN BURYING BEETLE

The American burying beetle is a striking-looking insect with a shiny black body and bright-orange markings on its head, wing covers, and at the ends of its two large antennae.

Beetle Brood

Burying beetles feed on the carcasses (dead bodies) of small birds and mammals. They also use carcasses to breed. A male and female first find a carcass and bury it in the soil. Then the female lays her eggs on it. When the eggs hatch a few days later, the larvae feed on the carcass, then burrow into the soil to **pupate**. The adult beetles emerge about a month later. They live for around a year.

An American burying beetle is caught in a bait bucket, ready to be monitored by conservationists.

Wild Fact Unusually for insects, American burying beetles are attentive parents. When the eggs hatch, both parents help to look after and feed the larvae until they can fend for themselves.

Vanishing Beetles

Only found in parts of North America, the burying beetle lives among grasslands, scrublands, and along the edges of forests. Records show that it was once common across Canada and the United States, but today it is only found in a few scattered populations. Scientists are not sure what has caused the beetle's decline, but habitat loss and the use of pesticides may be to blame.

An American burying beetle on animal fur. The beetles use their antennae to detect the smell of rotting flesh up to 2 miles away.

VITAL STATS

Scientific name:
Nicrophorus americanus

Body length: 1–2 in.

Diet: Dead birds and mammals

Numbers in the wild:
Unknown

Status: Critically endangered

Location: U.S. and Canada

Beetle Breeding

Conservationists are working hard to save the American burying beetle from extinction. Thousands of beetles have been bred in captivity at centers such as the Saint Louis Zoo in Missouri. The plan is to reintroduce these beetles back into the wild. In 2012, the first zoo-bred beetles were successfully released into southwest Missouri. To make the beetles feel at home, scientists dug holes at specially chosen sites and placed a bird carcass and a pair of beetles inside. Since then, these sites have been carefully monitored for signs of breeding activity, and the population seems to be growing.

ENDANGERED
OCEAN LIFE

OCEAN LIFE IN DANGER

This chapter looks at some of the most endangered sea animals. They have been chosen to show the variety of threats they face—from climate change or overfishing, to collisions with boats or theft of their eggs. The good news is that conservation groups and governments have been working to bring life back to many parts of our oceans. There is still much work to do, however.

WHAT IS OCEAN LIFE?

A huge variety of animals live in or on seas and oceans:
- Thousands of species of fish
- Mammals, such as whales
- Reptiles, such as crocodiles
- Birds, such as gulls and terns

A blue shark preys on a **shoal** of fish as part of a complex food chain.

A manta ray swims over a coral reef. Many of these rays die when they become entangled in fishing lines.

LOCATOR MAP: OCEAN LIFE

Blue whale

Largetooth sawfish

Knysna seahorse

Great hammerhead shark

Leatherback sea turtle

Mediterranean monk seal

Sea otter

Vaquita

Southern bluefin tuna

Commercial top shell

West Indian manatee

European eel

VAQUITA

The vaquita is a small, dark-gray **porpoise** with a white underside and dark rings around its mouth and eyes. It swims on its own or in small groups, feeding mainly on fish, squid, and crustaceans.

Vanishing Vaquita

The vaquita is found only in the Gulf of California, Mexico, where it lives in warm, shallow **lagoons** along the shore. Sadly, this rare and beautiful creature is the most endangered sea mammal in the world. In 2007, it was estimated that there were only around 150 vaquita left in the wild, putting it at serious risk of dying out. Since then, numbers have fallen further, and today there may be only around thirty vaquita left.

A vaquita calf comes to the surface to breathe.

This vaquita has been accidentally caught in a fishing net.

Fatal Fishing

The most serious threat facing the vaquita comes from fishing in the Gulf of California. The vaquita get accidentally caught up in fishing nets. They cannot reach the surface to breathe, and so they drown. The fish that most fishermen are illegally trying to catch is the totoaba. Like the vaquita, the totoaba is only found in the Gulf and is also critically endangered. It can be sold for large amounts of money in Asia.

Vaquita Rescue

Time is running out for the vaquita. Unless urgent action is taken, experts estimate that it could become extinct by 2025, if not before. In 2005, the Mexican Government set up the Vaquita Refuge in the Gulf, where the vaquita are protected and totoaba fishing is banned. Unfortunately, the fishing continues illegally, because the totoaba are so valuable. Conservationists and governments are working to bring about a ban on the trade in totoaba and find alternative ways for the fishermen to earn a living.

Totoaba are valuable fish, so fishermen are willing to break the law to catch them.

VITAL STATS

Scientific name:
Phocoena sinus

Length: 4–5 ft.

Diet: Fish, squid, crustaceans

Numbers in the wild:
Around 30

Status: Critically endangered

Location: Pacific Ocean

Wild Fact

A vaquita can be hard to spot because when it surfaces to breathe, it does so very slowly, hardly making a splash. Then it disappears again.

COMMERCIAL TOP SHELL

The commercial top shell is a species of sea snail—a type of mollusk. It is found in the Indian and Pacific Oceans, where it lives on rocks among coral reefs. It grazes on algae and other small plants.

Shell Life

The commercial top shell has a large shell, measuring up to 6 in. across its base. The shell is cone-shaped with cream and reddish-brown stripes. The snail inside has a large, pale-brown body, with a pair of long tentacles on its head. At **spawning time**, females release more than a million eggs, which are **fertilized** by the males. The eggs hatch into tiny larvae that drift on the ocean currents for two years before settling on rocks and turning into adults. Adults can live for up to fifteen years.

A commercial top shell can be seen here releasing its tiny green eggs.

Wild Fact Empty top shells have been found piled up on coral reefs. It seems that octopuses take them to a particular dining area to snack on!

Mother of Pearl

Once widespread in the Indian and Pacific Oceans, the commercial top shell has almost disappeared from the waters around several Pacific islands and is becoming rarer on many others. It is harvested for its meat and for its shell. A thick layer of **nacre** lines the insides of the shell and can be used to make mother-of-pearl buttons, beads, and pendants. Millions of pounds of these shells are collected and exported each year, bringing valuable income to many islanders.

Close-up of a commercial top shell. The inside of the shell is white and pearly.

VITAL STATS

Scientific name: *Tectus niloticus*

Height: Up to 7 in.

Diet: Algae

Numbers in the wild: Unknown

Status: Not currently classified

Location: Indian Ocean, Pacific Ocean

Commercial top shells are protected by law, but many are still harvested illegally.

Shell Survival

Today, overfishing is putting the commercial top shell at serious risk. So many shells have been taken that populations do not have time to recover. In addition, the coral reefs where they live are being destroyed by pollution, tourism, and tropical storms. Many countries across the top shells' range now reduce fishing for long periods of time to allow new shells to grow. Another priority is to turn the shells' reef habitats into protected marine reserves. There are also plans to release thousands of farmed shells into the wild to increase numbers.

BLUE WHALE

The blue whale is the biggest animal alive today. It can weigh 300,000 lbs. and grow up to 90 ft. long. Its heart alone is the size of a small car!

Big Eater

Despite its gigantic size, a blue whale mostly eats small, shrimplike crustaceans, called krill. It has an enormous appetite, however. In summer, when the krill form huge swarms, a whale may eat as much as 8,820 lbs. every day. Instead of teeth, it has bristly plates, called **baleen**, hanging down inside its mouth, which it uses to sieve the krill from the water.

A blue whale calf stays with its mother for the first year of its life.

Whale Hunting

Until the beginning of the twentieth century, the blue whale was found in every ocean, apart from the Arctic Ocean. But modern whaling equipment spelled disaster for the whales, which were hunted for their meat, oil, and bones. Hunting blue whales was banned in 1966, but the blue whale is still threatened by collisions with boats, ocean pollution, and getting tangled in fishing nets. Recently, numbers are thought to be increasing, but recovery is very slow. Before whaling, there were around 300,000 whales in the Southern Ocean. Today, there are between 10,000–25,000 worldwide.

Wild Fact

Blue whales have the deepest voices of any animal. Their "songs" can carry for hundreds of miles underwater, allowing them to communicate across the vast oceans.

VITAL STATS

Scientific name:
Balaenoptera musculus

Length: Around 82–90 ft.

Diet: Krill

Numbers in the wild: 10,000–25,000

Status: Endangered

Location: All oceans, except Arctic Ocean

A blue whale dives next to a whale-watching boat. Blue whales can hold their breath underwater for over twenty minutes.

Feeling Blue

Working alongside the International Whaling Commission, conservationists and governments have established Marine Protected Areas as sanctuaries for blue whales. In the eastern Pacific Ocean, the WWF has begun a project to fit satellite tags to a group of blue whales. This will allow them to track the whales and find out vital information about their movements and feeding patterns.

LEATHERBACK SEA TURTLE

The world's largest turtle, the leatherback, can measure more than 6 ft. long and weigh almost 2,210 lbs. It uses its long front flippers like paddles for propelling itself through the water.

Leatherback sea turtle hatchlings crawl toward the sea.

Beach Birth

Although the leatherback spends most of its time at sea, where it feeds on squid and jellyfish, females come ashore to breed. They use their back flippers to dig holes in the sand and lay around one hundred eggs inside. After about sixty days, the eggs hatch and the baby turtles dig their way out. They begin their short but dangerous journey to the sea, during which many are eaten by seabirds and crabs.

Turtle Trouble

Over the last twenty years, leatherback sea turtle numbers have fallen fast. Thousands of turtles are accidentally caught in fishing nets and drown because they cannot reach the surface to breathe. Thousands more are killed by eating plastic bags dumped in the sea, which the turtles mistake for jellyfish. Many vital nesting beaches are being destroyed by the building of tourist resorts, while tens of thousands of turtle eggs are illegally collected for food. In Malaysia, this has already led to the leatherback becoming extinct.

Beach Rescue

Conservation groups, such as the WWF and the
Leatherback Trust, are working to safeguard
the turtles' nesting beaches. In some places,
beaches have been set aside as sanctuaries
and are patrolled by teams of local rangers.
This has seen good results on beaches in
Costa Rica, where up to 100 percent of
turtle eggs used to be poached.

Turtle eggs in Indonesia
are **relocated** to a safer
nesting place.

Leatherback sea turtles
swim long distances
to reach their
breeding sites.

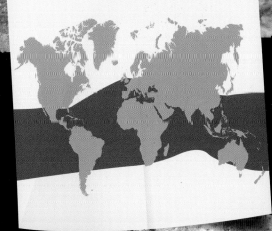

VITAL STATS

Scientific name:
Dermochelys coriacea

Length: Up to 6 ft.

Diet: Mostly jellyfish, squid

Numbers in the wild:
Around 2,300 (Pacific Ocean);
30,000 (Atlantic Ocean)

Status: Vulnerable

Location: Pacific Ocean,
Atlantic Ocean

Wild Fact
The leatherback
sea turtle can dive down to depths of over
3,280 ft.—deeper than any other turtle—
in search of jellyfish to eat. It can hold its
breath for up to eighty-five minutes.

SOUTHERN BLUEFIN TUNA

With its powerful, streamlined body, the southern bluefin tuna is one of the fastest fish in the sea. While the tuna usually cruises through the ocean at around 1–2 miles per hour, it is capable of reaching a staggering top speed over 40 miles per hour!

Tuna Travels

Southern bluefin tuna are among the biggest bony fish, growing up to 8 ft. long and weighing up to 440 lbs. They swim in large shoals, traveling vast distances from their breeding grounds in the Indian Ocean around Indonesia to their feeding grounds around southwestern Australia, where they eat smaller fish and squid.

Southern bluefin tuna gather in enormous shoals.

Taste for Tuna

Southern bluefin tuna are highly prized as food, especially in Japan. Thousands of pounds of tuna are caught every year, and a single fish can sell for thousands of dollars. Modern fishing fleets are equipped with high-tech satellites, **GPS**, and radar, which allow them to locate tuna shoals easily. Today, overfishing has pushed the southern bluefin tuna to the edge of extinction. Since the 1980s, its numbers have fallen by more than 90 percent.

Southern bluefin tuna are raised and fished on this farm in south Australia to reduce the numbers of wild tuna fished from the oceans.

VITAL STATS

Scientific name: *Thunnus maccoyii*

Length: Up to 8 ft.

Diet: Fish, squid, crustaceans

Numbers in the wild: Unknown

Status: Critically endangered

Location: Oceans in the Southern Hemisphere

Fishing Limits

Since the 1990s, many of the countries that fish for tuna have signed up to the Commission for the Conservation of the Southern Bluefin Tuna. This organization aims to protect the tuna, largely by placing strict limits on the numbers of tuna allowed to be caught. This should give the tuna time to recover, though many conservationists think that too little is being done too late.

Wild Fact Southern bluefin tuna can survive in cold water because their blood is specially adapted to hold heat, keeping their bodies warmer than the water around them.

GREAT HAMMERHEAD SHARK

Reaching up to 20 ft., this enormous shark is famous for its huge hammer-shaped head. Its eyes are located at either end of the hammer, with its mouth underneath. This unusual arrangement allows the shark to scan the ocean floor for food.

A great hammerhead shark swims off the Bahamas in the Atlantic Ocean.

Stingray Supper

Great hammerhead sharks are found along the coasts of warm seas around the world. They feed mainly on stingrays. The shark pins a stingray down on the sea floor with its hammer, then bites chunks from the ray's wings with its serrated, triangular teeth. Incredibly, most sharks aren't harmed by the venom in the stingray's tail spines, which are often found sticking inside their mouths.

Wild Fact

A great hammerhead hunts at dusk, swinging its head from side to side over the sea floor to pick up electrical signals from stingrays buried in the sand.

Shark Fin Soup

The main threat facing the great hammerhead is fishing. Its large, pointed back fin is used in Asia for making shark fin soup. Once the fin has been cut off, the rest of the shark is thrown back into the water, often alive. Without its fin, it cannot swim and therefore dies. Hammerhead sharks are also often accidentally caught in fishing nets because of the unique shape of their head.

Save a Shark

A great hammerhead shark can live for twenty to thirty years, but because it only breeds every two years, its numbers are declining. Some countries, including Australia and the United States, are now banning the removal of shark fins. Unfortunately, this practice continues illegally. In some places, such as the Bahamas, diving with hammerheads has become popular with tourists. Properly managed, it is hoped that this will help to raise awareness of the sharks and the need to protect them.

VITAL STATS

Scientific name:
Sphyrna mokarran
Length: Up to 20 ft.
Diet: Stingrays, fish
Numbers in the wild: Unknown
Status: Critically endangered
Location: Worldwide

A diver meets a great hammerhead shark.

MEDITERRANEAN MONK SEAL

One of the world's most endangered mammals, the Mediterranean monk seal was once widespread around the Mediterranean and Black Seas. Today, it only lives in a few small colonies off Greece, Turkey, and northern Africa.

Nursery Caves

The Mediterranean monk seal lives in warm water around the coast, where it spends the day foraging for fish, squid, and octopus. At breeding time, females come out of the sea to breed on sandy beaches or in rocky caves. They give birth to a single pup. Mother and pup have a strong bond and stay together for up to three years.

A Mediterranean monk seal swims in the sea near Portugal.

Struggling Seals

In ancient times, seeing a monk seal was thought to be lucky. Over the centuries, so many have been hunted for their skin, meat, and oil that they have almost disappeared. In the last fifty years alone, scientists estimate that seal numbers have fallen by around 60 percent. The seals are still hunted and killed by fishermen, who see them as competition for their catch. Pollution threatens their habitat in the busy Mediterranean Sea, and the coastlines along which they rest and breed are being developed for tourism.

A monk seal rests on a pebbly beach in Greece.

A researcher examines an orphaned seal pup in Izmir, Turkey.

VITAL STATS

Scientific name: *Monachus monachus*

Length: Up to 9.5 ft.

Diet: Fish, squid, octopus

Numbers in the wild: 250–350

Status: Endangered

Location: Atlantic Ocean, Mediterranean Sea

Action Plan

The Mediterranean monk seal is protected by law across its range, but urgent action is needed to save it. To protect the seals' breeding caves, monitored reserves have been set up. Observers are also being placed on boats to prevent the seals from getting tangled up in fishing gear. These measures seem to be working. In some countries where monk seals have been absent for a long time, such as Croatia, they have been spotted again.

Wild Fact Monk seals got their name because their smooth, brownish-gray coats were thought to look like a monk's robes.

KNYSNA SEAHORSE

The delicate Knysna (Cape) seahorse lives among thickets of **sea grass** up to 66 ft. below the surface of the water. Here, it is perfectly camouflaged by its mottled black-and-brown coloring. It grasps sea grass stalks with its tail to stop the current from carrying it away.

Caring Father

Seahorses are unusual fish because it is the male who carries the eggs until they hatch. During breeding, the female transfers her eggs to a pouch on the male's front. There, they grow and develop for two to three weeks until they hatch. Then the young swim out of the pouch, and their father leaves them to look after themselves.

Shrinking Range

Hundreds of thousands of Knysna seahorses once lived along the south coast of South Africa. Sadly, their numbers have fallen by half in the last ten years, and today they are only found in the **estuaries** of three rivers. Some are poached for the pet trade or to be used in alternative medicines, but the fall in their numbers is mainly due to the loss of their habitat, as more people move to live along the coast. Waste water and sewage pollute the water, and boats damage the sea grass beds.

The Knysna seahorse is caught and used for alternative medicines. It is thought to help treat asthma and some skin problems.

VITAL STATS

Scientific name:
Hippocampus capensis

Length: Around 4 in.

Diet: Small crustaceans

Numbers in the wild:
Fewer than 100,000

Status: Endangered

Location: Atlantic Ocean

Save the Seahorse

The first seahorse to be declared endangered, the Knysna seahorse is now protected by law in South Africa. Several projects, such as the Knysna Seahorse Status Project, have been started to protect the seahorse and get local people involved in saving it. There are captive-breeding programs at the Two Oceans Aquarium in Cape Town and Belgium's Antwerp Zoo. This captive-bred stock will be used to supply aquaria and the pet trade, to keep seahorses from being poached from the wild.

Wild Fact Knysna seahorses feed on small crustaceans that live on sea grass stalks. They do not have stomachs and their digestive system processes food so quickly that they need to eat almost nonstop.

LARGETOOTH SAWFISH

Belonging to the same group of bony fish as sharks, skates, and rays, the largetooth sawfish lives along the coasts of tropical oceans. It can also survive in freshwater rivers and lakes.

A largetooth sawfish lies on the sea bottom in Australia.

Super Saw

One of the world's largest fish, the largetooth sawfish can grow up to 23 ft. long. Its long sawlike mouth makes up to a quarter of its length, and the edges are lined with long, sharp teeth. The sawfish is a predator, feeding on fish, crustaceans, and mollusks. It uses its saw to slash at shoals of fish and to dig up sand and mud to find prey. Young sawfish hatch from eggs inside their mother. To protect her, their saws are soft and bendy, and their teeth do not harden until after their birth.

Vanishing Fast

The largetooth sawfish was once widespread in warmer parts of the Atlantic and Pacific Oceans. Today, it is extinct or very rare across much of its range. It is hunted for its fins, which are made into shark fin soup, and for its saws, which are sold as ornaments. Their saw is also easily entangled in fishing nets. In Australia, fishermen are required by law to release the sawfish alive, but these large fish can be difficult to handle and often die anyway.

Save a Sawfish

Without urgent action, it seems unlikely that the largetooth sawfish will survive. In 2012, conservationists from around the world met in London to address the sawfishes' plight. International trade in sawfish body parts is now banned, and work is being done to find out more about the fish, especially how they breed. In some places, such as Australia, the sawfish are protected, but this is not yet the case everywhere.

VITAL STATS

Scientific name: *Pristis pristis*

Length: Up to 23 ft.

Diet: Small fish, crustaceans

Numbers in the wild: Unknown

Status: Critically endangered

Location: Atlantic Ocean, Pacific Ocean

Conservationists examine a largetooth sawfish.

 **Wild fact** The "teeth" on a sawfish's saw are not actually teeth but a type of scale. The sawfish's real teeth are inside its mouth, which is located on its underside.

SEA OTTER

Sea otters are well adapted for life in the sea. Their large back feet work like flippers, and they steer with their rudder-like tails. Their thick fur coats keep them warm and dry.

Upside-down Otter

A sea otter dives to the sea bed to find sea urchins, mussels, and crabs to eat. It carries them to the surface in pouches of skin under its armpits. Then it lies on its back and uses its chest as a table to open the shells, sometimes smashing them with a rock. Pups are also carried on the female's chest, while she nurses them and grooms their fur.

A sea otter cares for her pup off the coast of California.

Wild Fact California sea otters sleep on their backs in the water. They wind strands of seaweed around their bodies to stop themselves from drifting away on ocean currents.

Fatal Fur Trade

Once found in large numbers along the North Pacific coasts of Russia and the United States, sea otters were hunted almost to extinction for their highly prized fur. By 1900, there were fewer than 2,000 left, down from hundreds of thousands a century earlier. Worst hit were the California otters, whose numbers fell as low as fifty. Today, sea otter numbers have risen again, but they are still extremely rare and are threatened by ocean pollution, oil spills, and entanglement in fishing gear.

Sea otters float in the waters off Alaska.

A rescued sea otter pup at Monterey Bay Aquarium in California is wrapped in fake kelp to prepare it for being released back into the wild.

VITAL STATS

Scientific name:
Enhydra lutris

Body length: Around 5 ft.

Diet: Sea urchins, mussels, crabs

Numbers in the wild:
Around 125,000

Status: Endangered

Location: Pacific Ocean

Sea Otter Rescue

Sea otters are now protected, and many conservation organizations are working on their behalf. At the Monterey Bay Aquarium in California, stranded or injured otters are rescued and nursed back to health. Radio transmitters are fitted to track them once they are released back into the wild. This information helps scientists understand the threats to the sea otters and work toward the species' recovery.

EUROPEAN EEL

A long, snakelike fish, the European eel can grow up to 5 ft. long. It is unusual because it spends part of its life in fresh water and part in the sea.

An adult European eel swims down the River Rhône in France.

Eel Travelers

A European eel spawns in the Sargasso Sea in the North Atlantic Ocean. The eggs hatch into larvae that look like curled leaves. For the next three years, the larvae drift on the ocean currents toward the coasts of Europe. After the larvae hatch, the young eels swim up rivers and spend up to twenty years growing into adults. As adults, they travel thousands of miles back to the sea to lay their eggs. They can live for up to eighty-five years.

Wild Fact
Eels change color as they mature. Elvers (young eels) are so transparent that you could read a book through them! Adult eels are black, brown, or dark green.

Edible Eels

Eels used to be common in Europe, but their numbers have fallen by up to 95 percent in the last twenty-five years. In some places, they have disappeared completely. The main threat comes from overfishing—eels are a very popular food in Asia and Europe. Dams and weirs are also increasingly blocking the eels' migration routes and preventing the young eels from being able to swim up the rivers, where they mature. This problem may get worse as more hydroelectric projects are built along rivers.

Young eels are released into a lake in Wales.

VITAL STATS

Scientific name:
Anguilla anguilla

Length: Up to 5 ft.

Diet: Mollusks, crustaceans, fish

Numbers in the wild: Unknown

Status: Critically endangered

Location: Atlantic Ocean and European rivers

Eel Lifeline

Already critically endangered, urgent action is needed to save the European eel from extinction. An international recovery plan has been launched, and strict limits have been put on eel fishing. In England and Wales, the Environment Agency has built "eel ladders" on some rivers. These are ramps and steps that help the eels swim past obstacles, such as dams. On other rivers, young eels are trapped, then released farther upstream once they are clear of barriers. The eels are also tagged to help scientists better understand their movements.

A young eel wriggles up an eel ladder as it swims upstream.

WEST INDIAN MANATEE

More closely related to elephants than to whales, a manatee is a large, round sea mammal with a bristly snout. Its front limbs are short and flipper-like, and it uses its tail like a paddle.

A West Indian manatee calf will stay with its mother for one to two years.

Manatee Lifestyle

The West Indian manatee lives along the coasts of the eastern United States, Gulf of Mexico, and Caribbean Sea. It spends hours at a time grazing on sea grass that grows under the water, coming to the surface to breathe every few minutes. Manatees have to venture up rivers and creeks to get freshwater for drinking. They can live for more than fifty years, but only have one calf every two years.

Fatal Collisions

In the past, the greatest danger facing the manatee was being hunted for its meat, oil, and skin. Today, most manatee deaths are caused by collisions with boats and Jet Skis. Manatees also get tangled in fishing gear and are suffering from habitat loss.

VITAL STATS

Scientific name:
Trichechus manatus

Length: Up to 13 ft.

Diet: Sea grass

Numbers in the wild:
More than 6,000

Status: Vulnerable

Location: Atlantic Ocean

Wild Fact
When a manatee's molar teeth get old or worn out, new teeth grow up in the back of its jaws and push forward to replace them. This can happen many times over the course of its life.

An orphaned West Indian manatee calf is bottle-fed at the Manatee Rehabilitation Center in Belize.

Road to Recovery

By the 1970s, there were only a few hundred West Indian manatees left in the wild. Thanks to a range of conservation measures, numbers have now increased to more than 6,000. In the United States, manatee protection areas have been set up, with signs warning boat operators to slow down. There are also plans in place for recycling fishing lines, rather than dumping them in the water. The manatees in the protected areas are carefully monitored and given regular health checks.

ENDANGERED REPTILES

REPTILES IN DANGER

Around one in five of the world's species of reptiles is facing extinction today. They face threats from hunters who kill them either for meat or to sell their body parts, and from "exotic pet" traders who sell reptiles to be kept in people's homes.

The American alligator was brought back from the brink of extinction.

The Santa Catalina Island rattlesnake is critically endangered. Feral cats prey on the snake. It is also collected for the pet trade.

WHAT ARE REPTILES?

- Vertebrates
- Cold-blooded
- Most lay eggs
- Have scales
- Have four legs or no legs

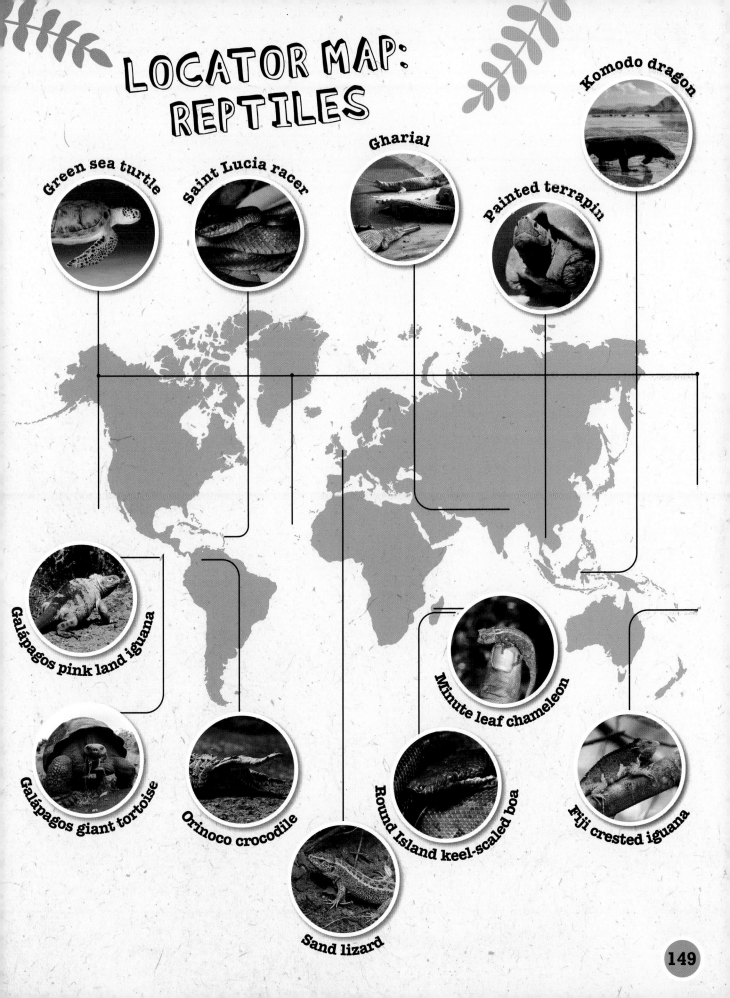

LOCATOR MAP: REPTILES

Komodo dragon

Green sea turtle

Saint Lucia racer

Gharial

Painted terrapin

Galápagos pink land iguana

Minute leaf chameleon

Galápagos giant tortoise

Orinoco crocodile

Round Island keel-scaled boa

Fiji crested iguana

Sand lizard

GREEN SEA TURTLE

One of the largest sea turtles, the green sea turtle is found in tropical and subtropical waters in the Atlantic, Indian, and Pacific Oceans. It feeds on sea grass and algae, which turns the fat beneath its shell green, giving the turtle its name.

Wild Fact

Baby green sea turtles have a special hooked "egg tooth" on their jaws that they use to break out of their eggs. The egg tooth later falls off.

A green sea turtle swims in the warm waters of the Caribbean Sea.

Green sea turtle babies crawl from their nests toward the sea.

Long Journey

Each year, adult green sea turtles make long journeys to breed on sandy beaches. Some swim 1,400 miles across the Atlantic Ocean, from Brazil to Ascension Island. At night, the females haul themselves up the shore and use their back flippers to dig deep nests in the sand. They lay up to 200 eggs, then cover them with sand. The eggs hatch about two months later, and the baby turtles crawl toward the sea. This is a dangerous time for the turtles—many are eaten by gulls and crabs before they reach the water.

Turtle Threats

The green sea turtle faces many threats, and its numbers are falling fast. Each year, thousands of turtles are accidentally caught up in fishing equipment and therefore drown. Others are entangled in the plastic that litters the ocean. Thousands more green sea turtles are hunted for their meat and eggs. Their nesting beaches are also polluted by tourism and other human activities.

VITAL STATS

Scientific name: *Chelonia mydas*
Length: Up to 5 ft.
Weight: Up to 660 lbs.
Diet: Seagrass, algae
Numbers in the wild: Unknown
Status: Endangered
Location: Tropical and subtropical oceans

This green sea turtle is being weighed and checked by a scientist.

Turtle Rescue

There are many laws in place to stop the trade in and hunting of green sea turtles and their eggs. Locally, conservationists are working hard to clean up and protect the turtles' nesting beaches. They also campaign to limit the amount of building near nest sites, set up safe refuges for the turtles, and reduce artificial lighting, which **disorients** the baby turtles as they leave their nests and head to sea. Teams of rangers patrol the beaches to guard them from poachers.

SAINT LUCIA RACER

One of the rarest snakes in the world, the Saint Lucia racer was declared extinct in 1936. However, in the following years, several Saint Lucia racers were spotted on the tiny Caribbean island of Maria Major.

A Saint Lucia racer resting among leaf litter.

Snake Secrets

The Saint Lucia racer is a small light-brown snake with a dark-brown zigzag pattern running along its back. True to its name, it can move fast! It feeds on frogs and lizards, and may steal eggs from lizards' burrows.

Wild Fact

Like other similar snakes, the Saint Lucia racer's lower jaw has two parts, allowing it to open wide to swallow large prey.

The nature reserve of Maria Major island is less than a mile from Saint Lucia and is at risk from invasive species.

VITAL STATS

Scientific name:
Erythrolamprus ornatus

Body length: Up to 3.5 ft.

Diet: Frogs, lizards, lizard eggs

Numbers in the wild: Approx. 18

Status: Critically endangered

Location: Maria Major, Caribbean

Risk and Rescue

Once widespread on Maria Major's larger neighbor, Saint Lucia, the racer was wiped out by Asian **mongooses** brought over to the island by settlers. Today, scientists estimate there may be only eighteen racers left in the wild. Because their range is so small, a single event, such as a drought or tropical storm, could mean extinction.

A New Home

Conservationists are trying to work out the best way to save the snakes. One plan is to breed the snakes in captivity, then release them into another location, such as tiny Dennery Island, also off Saint Lucia. But first, they would have to remove the island's goats so that the plant life could recover, restoring the racers' habitat, and then bring over some lizards as prey for the snakes.

GHARIAL

Gharials are large crocodilians from India and Nepal that can grow up to 20 ft. long. They have very long, narrow jaws filled with razor-sharp teeth.

Stealthy Hunter

Gharials live along deep, fast-flowing rivers, where they hunt for fish. Lurking in the water, a gharial whips its head sideways to snap up its prey with its teeth. The long, narrow shape of the gharial's jaws means they cut quickly through the water.

The gharial's 110 needlelike, interlocking teeth are perfect for capturing their prey.

An Indian gharial at the water's edge.

Under Threat

The gharial was once found across southern Asia. Today, it is only found in a few places along rivers in northern India and Nepal. The main threat to gharials is habitat loss, as the human population grows bigger and rivers are used for water, to generate hydroelectricity, and for fishing. Local fishermen kill the gharials because they see them as rivals for their catch, and gharials are also hunted for their eggs.

These gharials have been reared under a protection program.

VITAL STATS

Scientific name: *Gavialis gangeticus*

Length: Up to 20 ft.

Diet: Fish

Numbers in the wild: 200–250

Status: Critically endangered

Location: India, Nepal

Rescue Mission

By the 1970s, fewer than 200 gharials were left in the wild, and a captive-breeding program was launched. But by 2006, poaching and habitat loss had again reduced the number to fewer than 200 adults. Led by the Gharial Conservation Alliance, conservationists are focusing on protecting the gharials' habitat and helping local people to better understand them.

Wild Fact A gharial has such weak legs that when it is on land, it cannot raise its body off the ground.

ROUND ISLAND KEEL-SCALED BOA

Found only on Round Island, near Mauritius in the Indian Ocean, the very rare Round Island keel-scaled boa has a slender dark-brown and cream body. It is covered in keeled (ridged) scales that give the snake its name.

The Round Island keel-scaled boa's scales give its skin a rough surface.

Life in the Trees

Scientists are still trying to find out more about this secretive snake. It is mainly nocturnal, coming out at night to hunt for its prey of lizards, and spends some of its life in the trees. At breeding time, the female lays a clutch of around twelve eggs in a hollow tree trunk or among leaf litter. The eggs take about three months to hatch, when tiny, bright-orange young emerge.

Habitat Horror

Round Island was once covered in forest and palm groves where the keel-scaled boa thrived. Sadly, rabbits and goats brought to the island many years ago by settlers destroyed much of this habitat. By the 1970s, there were only around fifty snakes left. The rabbits and goats have now been removed, and the island's vegetation has grown back. This has helped the island's lizard population increase, providing prey for the snakes. The island is now a wildlife reserve, and the number of boas has steadily increased to over 1,000.

The keel-scaled boa at night, when its skin is a lighter color.

VITAL STATS

Scientific name:
Casarea dussumieri

Body length: Around 5 ft.

Diet: Lizards

Numbers in the wild:
Around 1,500

Status: Vulnerable

Location: Round Island

New Homes

Working with the Mauritian Wildlife Foundation, conservationists from Jersey Zoo are leading the campaign to safeguard the boas' future. In 2012, sixty snakes were relocated to the tiny nearby island of Gunner's Quoin. The island was cleared of rats and hares, and screened for disease. Hundreds of lizards were introduced as prey. A year later, the first young boas were spotted, showing that the snakes were breeding successfully.

Wild Fact The Round Island keel-scaled boa's skin is specialized to change color, from dark during the day when it is resting, to lighter at night when it is awake.

GALÁPAGOS GIANT TORTOISE

The Galápagos giant tortoise is the world's largest tortoise and one of the longest-lived vertebrates in the world, living for well over one hundred years in the wild. It is found on the Galápagos Islands, 620 miles off the coast of Ecuador.

Tortoises first arrived on the Galápagos Islands around 3 million years ago.

Tortoise Life

Galápagos tortoises mostly eat cacti, leaves, and grass. The size and shape of their shell varies, depending on what they eat. Saddle-backed tortoises have a curve at the front of their shells so they can stretch their necks up to reach taller plants. Dome-shelled tortoises cannot raise their heads and so graze on plants nearer to the ground. When the tortoises are not feeding, they rest for up to sixteen hours a day.

Tortoise in Trouble

As many as 300,000 giant tortoises once roamed the Galápagos Islands. From the nineteenth century, sailors and settlers began hunting them for food and oil. They also brought goats, pigs, and rats to the islands that preyed on the tortoises and their eggs, and overgrazed their habitat. By the middle of the twentieth century, tortoise numbers had been reduced by around 90 percent.

A baby Galápagos giant tortoise at a breeding center in the Galápagos.

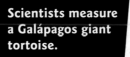

Scientists measure a Galápagos giant tortoise.

Road to Recovery

In 1959, the islands were declared a national park and a program was put in place to save the tortoises. Some eggs were moved, and the baby tortoises were raised in captivity until they were too big to be eaten by rats. They were then put back into the wild. Thousands of goats and, later, rats were removed from the islands. Captive-bred tortoises are also being reintroduced to islands whose wild tortoises had become extinct.

VITAL STATS

Scientific name:
Chelonoidis nigra complex
(includes 12 species)

Length: Up to 5 ft.

Weight: Up to 710 lbs.

Diet: Cacti, grass, leaves, berries

Numbers in the wild: About 20,000

Status: Critically endangered, Endangered, or Vulnerable, depending on species

Location: Galápagos Islands

Wild Fact The Galápagos giant tortoise can survive for a year without water. It lives on water stored in its bladder and at the base of its neck.

FIJI CRESTED IGUANA

The Fiji crested iguana is a large bright-green lizard with narrow white bands and a spiny crest along its back. It lives in small patches of dry, tropical forest on a few of the islands that make up Fiji in the South Pacific Ocean.

A Fiji crested iguana resting on a tree branch.

A hibiscus flower is a tasty treat for the Fiji crested iguana.

Iguana Behavior

Moving through the forest trees, the Fiji crested iguana grips the trunks and branches with its long claws and tail. It mainly feeds on leaves and flowers. If it is threatened by a predator, it can quickly change color from green to black.

Greedy Goats

This stunning reptile faces many dangers. Many local people are afraid of it because of its dramatic color change when it is threatened. But the biggest threat is to its habitat, which is being cleared for farming and destroyed by fires, storms, and wild goats. On one island, precious forest was bulldozed to build a luxury tourist resort.

VITAL STATS

Scientific name:
Brachylophus vitiensis
Length: 2–3 ft.
Diet: Mainly leaves and flowers
Numbers in the wild:
Estimated 1,200–1,400
Status: Critically endangered
Location: Fiji

Wild Fact When threatened, the Fiji crested iguana stretches out its neck, bobs its head, and pounces to scare its enemy away.

Fiji crested iguanas are now bred in captivity for release into the wild.

Habitat Repair

As part of a captive-breeding program led by the National Trust for Fiji, the small island of Yadua Taba was cleared of goats in 1981 and declared a national sanctuary for the iguanas. Large parts of the forest have recovered, creating a safe habitat for a group of iguanas. Unfortunately, at present Yadua Taba is the only island that is being monitored, and more work needs to be done.

KOMODO DRAGON

Growing to around 10 ft. long, the Komodo dragon is the largest and heaviest lizard in the world. It is found on a few volcanic islands in Indonesia, including Komodo.

A Komodo dragon walks along a beach in Komodo National Park.

Killer Komodo

Komodo dragons eat almost any kind of meat, including animals as large as water buffalo. They detect their prey by sight and smell, flicking out their long, yellow, forked tongues to pick up the scent. The dragon grabs its prey with its sharp claws, then tears off chunks of flesh with its large, serrated teeth. A Komodo dragon can eat up to three quarters of its body weight in one sitting.

Baby dragons climb trees to avoid being eaten by predators.

Researchers catch a Komodo dragon to measure and tag.

Fragile Habitat

The Komodo dragon faces many threats, including volcanic eruptions, earthquakes, and poaching. Its habitat is also being damaged by pollution and poisonous chemicals used in fishing. In 1980, the Komodo National Park was set up to protect the dragons and their habitat. In 1991, the park was declared a UNESCO World Heritage Site.

Captive Komodos

Komodo dragons have been kept in captivity since 1927. Their keepers report that they can become quite tame and recognize their own keeper. Captive-breeding programs have had mixed success. However, in 1992, thirteen baby dragons hatched from eggs at the Smithsonian National Zoo in Washington, D.C. They were the first Komodo dragons to be born outside Indonesia.

VITAL STATS

Scientific name:
Varanus komodoensis

Length: Up to 10 ft.

Weight: Usually up to 200 lbs., but can reach more than 300 lbs.

Diet: Deer, wild pigs, water buffalo, young Komodo

Numbers in the wild: About 3,000

Status: Vulnerable

Location: Indonesia

Wild Fact A Komodo dragon's bite is not only venomous, stopping its victim's blood from clotting, but its **saliva** also contains deadly **bacteria**.

163

ORINOCO CROCODILE

The Orinoco crocodile lives along the banks of the Orinoco River in Colombia and Venezuela. A fearsome predator, it can grow up to 16 ft. long. Despite its size, it is one of South America's most endangered species.

Wild Fact

An Orinoco crocodile's nostrils are at the end of its snout. When the crocodile is lying in the water, its nostrils stay above the surface so it can still breathe.

An Orinoco crocodile basking on the riverbank in Venezuela.

Caring Mothers

In the dry season, Orinoco crocodiles dig burrows in the riverbank, where they lay around forty eggs. They stay close to their nests, guarding the eggs from vultures and lizards. Three months later, the eggs start to hatch. Inside, the babies make squeaking calls to alert their mother, who then takes them to water. She carries them carefully in her mouth, without shutting her jaw fully, to avoid hurting them with her sharp teeth. She may look after them for up to three years.

A young Orinoco crocodile.

Crocodile Crisis

The Orinoco crocodile was once found across Colombia and Venezuela, but today there are only around 1,500 left. Between the 1930s and 1960s, it was hunted almost to extinction for its skin. Despite being a protected species, the crocodile is still hunted illegally, and young crocodiles are captured for the exotic pet trade. Pollution, farming, and dam-building are also destroying its habitat.

VITAL STATS

Scientific name:
Crocodylus intermedius

Length: Up to 16 ft.

Weight: Up to 840 lbs.

Diet: Fish, birds, small mammals

Numbers in the wild:
Up to about 1,500

Status: Critically endangered

Location: Colombia and Venezuela

Croc Conservation

A captive-breeding program for the crocodiles is underway in Venezuela, and since the early 1990s, young crocodiles have been put back into the wild on private ranches and in national parks. In 2014, the Orinoco crocodile also became part of a project to protect ten endangered species that share its habitat.

A young Orinoco crocodile is released into the wild.

MINUTE LEAF CHAMELEON

Measuring up to 1.5 in. long, the minute leaf chameleon is one of the smallest reptiles in the world. It is only found in a few patches of rain forest in Madagascar.

Life in the Leaves

The chameleon has a row of spiny scales running down each side of its spine and is colored green, brown, and gray, often with black stripes. This helps camouflage it as it hunts for tiny insects in the leaf litter on the forest floor. It climbs onto a branch to sleep. If a predator approaches, the chameleon drops to the forest floor and plays dead.

The minute leaf chameleon looks like a piece of dead wood on the ground, so predators leave it alone.

Hard to Find

The minute leaf chameleon lives in parts of northern Madagascar—on the mainland and on the island of Nosy Be. Scientists cannot tell for certain how many of these delicate reptiles are left in the wild, but they do know that the chameleon is disappearing fast. The biggest threat it faces is habitat loss. The few remaining areas of its forest home are being cleared at an alarming rate by **slash-and-burn** farming and by cutting down trees to turn into **charcoal** for fuel.

Rival Reptiles

Although the chameleon is protected in several nature reserves, its future is still uncertain. Much more work is needed, especially to involve local people who rely on the forest for their living. However, there is a lot of interest in the chameleon, and scientists are making exciting discoveries all the time. They have even found a new, even smaller species of chameleon: the *Brookesia micra*.

The chameleons' forest habitat is being burned down.

The minute leaf chameleon easily sits on a person's thumb.

VITAL STATS

Scientific name:
Brookesia minima

Length: Up to 1.5 in.

Diet: Insects

Numbers in the wild: Unknown

Status: Endangered

Location: Madagascar

Wild Fact A chameleon's eyes can move and focus independently from each other. This means they can look at two different objects at the same time!

SAND LIZARD

The sand lizard is a stocky reptile with brown, scaly skin. Males turn bright green in the breeding season. It lives on sandy heaths and sand dunes along the coast in parts of Europe and the U.K.

Sun Bathing

The sand lizard's color helps camouflage it from birds and other predators, but at night it burrows into the sand to hide from its enemies. In winter, it hibernates in a long, narrow burrow in the dunes, then emerges in spring to breed. In June and July, the female lays up to fourteen eggs under the sand. The young lizards hatch one to two months later.

A baby sand lizard hatching from its egg.

Sinking Sands

Today, the sand lizard is extremely rare in the U.K. and found only in a few isolated sites. Over the last 200 years, almost two thirds of its habitat has been lost. Some has been turned into farmland; some used for building houses; and some excavated for sand. This has had a devastating effect on the sand lizard populations in the U.K.

A female sand lizard guards her nest burrow.

New Homes

To safeguard the sand lizards, several wildlife organizations in the U.K. are working to protect the reptiles' habitat and create new places for them to live. Once a suitable site is prepared, they plan to introduce captive-bred lizards back into the wild. In 2018, twenty-one sand lizards were released onto specially made sand banks in Farnham Heath, Surrey in the U.K. Another eighty-six lizards were released in Farnborough, Hampshire, also in the U.K. Some of the lizards were fitted with radio tags, so conservationists could track their movements.

Wild Fact A sand lizard can shed its tail if a predator grabs it. It then grows a new one, which is thin, black, and shiny at first.

This male sand lizard has grown a new tail.

PAINTED TERRAPIN

A very rare river turtle, the painted terrapin lives in Southeast Asia in mangrove swamps and estuaries. Its gray-brown shell blends in well with its muddy habitat. It mostly feeds on the fruits, shoots, and leaves of riverside plants.

River to Sea

The painted terrapin gets its name from the splashes of red and white that appear on a male's head to attract a mate. During the breeding season, female terrapins travel down the river to the sea. Here, they dig holes in sandy beaches or sandbanks and lay around ten to twelve eggs at a time. The eggs hatch around three months later, and the young terrapins head back to the river on their own.

Terrapin Threats

Today, painted terrapins are only found along a few rivers in Malaysia and Indonesia. Their greatest threat comes from poachers hunting for terrapin eggs, which are eaten in many parts of Asia. Their habitat is also being destroyed to make space for fish and shrimp farms, and for palm oil plantations.

Female painted terrapins are larger than males.

Beach Patrol

The painted terrapin is protected in Malaysia. Egg collectors must have special licenses and sell a large part of their haul to the Malaysian Fisheries Department to be hatched and returned to the wild. Conservationists are also working to save the terrapins. Instead of earning money from selling eggs, local people are being trained to carry out patrols of nesting beaches and collect vital information. Painted terrapins are also being bred in captivity and released into the wild.

A male painted terrapin with red-and-white markings.

VITAL STATS

Scientific name: *Batagur borneoensis*

Shell size: 28 in. long, 17 in. wide (female)

Diet: Riverside plants

Numbers in the wild: Unknown

Status: Critically endangered

Location: Southeast Asia

Wild Fact Painted terrapins are well adapted to life in the river. They have streamlined shells, webbed feet for swimming, and pointed snouts that act like snorkels.

GALÁPAGOS PINK LAND IGUANA

This striking iguana has a crest along its back and sharp claws on its back legs. It looks pink because it has no pigment in its skin, so the color of its blood shows through.

Volcano Visit

The Galápagos pink land iguana is only found on the slopes of Wolf Volcano on Isabela Island, which is part of the Galápagos Islands. It was first spotted by park rangers in 1986 and officially identified as a new species in 2009. The iguanas feed mainly on the prickly pear cactus, but scientists are still trying to find out more about how they have adapted to their harsh habitat.

The Galápagos pink land iguana is protected by a thick layer of rosy scales.

Wild Fact A male pink iguana bobs its head up and down very quickly—about once every second—when trying to attract a female for breeding.

An iguana feeding on fruits and leaves.

The Wolf Volcano on Isabela Island is still active.

VITAL STATS

Scientific name:
Conolophus marthae
Length: Up to 4 ft.
Diet: Prickly pear leaves and fruit
Numbers in the wild: Around 200
Status: Critically endangered
Location: Galápagos Islands

Facing Danger

Today, there are around 200 of these unusual iguanas in the wild, and they are in grave danger. Introduced predators, such as rats and cats, prey on their eggs and young. They are also at risk of being wiped out by drought. But the biggest threat comes from the nearby Wolf Volcano. It last erupted in 2015, but luckily the lava flowing from the volcano missed the iguanas' territory.

Taking Action

Because the number of iguanas is so small, it is very vulnerable. The iguana is protected by law in the wild, but a captive-breeding program has also been started to safeguard the species' future. The plan is to establish another population on another island that has been cleared of rats and cats.

GLOSSARY

abdomen the middle part of an insect's body

algae tiny plants

amphibians animals that usually spend part of their life in water and part on land

antennae long, thin feelers often found on an insect's head

bacteria tiny, single-celled living things that lack a nucleus

baleen rows of bony plates that hang down inside some whales' mouths

biodiversity the variety of plants and animals that live in the world or in a particular habitat

camouflage the natural coloring, patterns, or shape of an animal that help it blend in with its surroundings

captive-breeding program when endangered animals are bred in captivity, zoos, or wildlife reserves

carcasses bodies of a dead animals

charcoal a black, coal-like material made by burning wood

chytridiomycosis a disease that affects amphibians around the world. It is caused by a fungus and can spread very quickly between animals. The disease has already killed around a third of the world's amphibians. So far, there is no known cure

climate change the way in which weather patterns on Earth change over a long period

cold-blooded relating to an animal whose body temperature varies with that of its surroundings

colony a group of animals that live together

conservationists scientists or other people who work to protect endangered wildlife and habitats

crustaceans animals, such as lobsters, shrimp, or crabs, that have a hard shell and mostly live in the sea

deciduous describing trees that shed their leaves, then grow them back every year

decoy something used to mislead or trick an animal into a trap

deforestation the cutting down and clearing of a large area of forest

disorients causes an animal to lose its way or direction

domestic an animal that has been tamed and is kept as a pet or farm animal

dormant having normal activity slowed down to conserve energy

endangered in danger of becoming extinct

entomologists people who study insects

erosion the way in which the wind and water wear away the landscape

estuaries the mouths of large rivers, where the tide meets the stream

evaporates turns from liquid into vapor or gas

evolution the process by which different living things have developed over thousands or millions of years

excretes removes waste from the body

extinction when an animal or plant has died out forever

fertilized when a male has added his sperm to a female's egg so that young can grow

forage to search an area for food

fungal describing a fungus or a disease caused by a fungus

gills part of a fish or other animal's body that is used for breathing underwater. Gills take in oxygen dissolved in the water

global warming a gradual increase in the temperature of Earth's atmosphere, largely because of human activities, such as burning fossil fuels (oil, gas, and coal)

gorge a narrow valley with steep, rocky walls through which a stream runs

GPS (Global Positioning System) a system that uses satellites to fix locations and draw up accurate maps

habitat the natural home of an animal or plant

hand-reared an animal that is raised by a person, away from its parents

herbicides chemicals used for killing plants, especially weeds

hydroelectric describing something that makes electricity using flowing water

hyraxes small mammals with short legs and tails with hooflike toes

immune to be protected from a disease, naturally or medically

incubating when a bird is sitting on its eggs to keep them warm and help them hatch

infectious a disease that can be spread between people and/or other living things

insecticide a chemical used for killing insects

invertebrates animals that do not have bony backbones inside their bodies

irrigation supplying water to fields or crops to help them grow

keratin a hard material found in nails, claws, horns, and feathers

lagoons shallow ponds near or linked to a larger body of water

larvae the often wormlike young that hatch from the eggs of many insects

leaf litter the deep layer of dead and rotting leaves on the forest floor

marsupials mammals with a pouch in which young develop and grow

migration a journey taken by an animal, often between their breeding and feeding grounds

mollusks animals, such as snails, squid, or octopuses, with soft bodies

mongooses slender mammals that feed on snakes, birds, and eggs

nacre another word for mother-of-pearl

nocturnal an animal that comes out to look for food at night

overgrazing when a piece of land is grazed (fed on) by too many animals

peat a marshy soil made from partly rotten plants

pesticides chemicals used to kill plants or animals that are considered pests

pigment a chemical that colors an animal's skin

plantations large-scale farms that grow crops, such as palm oil, sugar, rubber, or coffee

plateau a raised area of land with a level surface

poaching when animals are illegally hunted and/or caught

pollinate to transfer pollen from one flower to another, or one part of a flower to another, so that seeds and new plants can grow

porpoise a sea mammal related to whales and dolphins

predators animals that hunt and kill other animals for food

prey an animal that is hunted and killed by another animal for food

pupae the stage between larvae and adult insects, enclosed in a cocoon, chrysalis, or other protective covering

pupate to become a pupa—the form between a larva and an adult insect

range the area or areas over which an animal is found

regurgitate to bring up food that has been swallowed

relocated moved to another place

reptiles cold-blooded animals with scaly skin that usually lay eggs

ruff a ring of feathers that sticks up around a bird's neck

saliva a watery liquid made in an animal's mouth

sea grass a plant with narrow, grasslike leaves that grows in shallow coastal waters

serrated having a jagged edge

shoal large group of fish

slash-and-burn a method of agriculture where vegetation is cut down and burned before new seeds are sown

spawning time the time of year when fish and other animals produce their young

species a category of related living things that can interbreed

thermals currents of warm air that rise upward

translucent clear or transparent

unfertilized when no male has added his sperm to a female's egg, so the eggs will not grow into young

vaccine a medicine used to protect humans or animals from diseases

vertebrates animals that have a backbone inside their bodies

vulnerable likely to be harmed or hurt

warm-blooded having a relatively high, constant internally regulated body temperature relatively independent of the surroundings

wetlands areas made up of swamps, marshes, and boggy land

wildlife sanctuary a safe area where wildlife is protected from poaching, hunting, and habitat destruction

INDEX